Data Governance
Needs
Risk Management

Moving from
Data-driven to Business-driven

Mark Atkins

Terry Smith

Technics Publications

TECHNICS PUBLICATIONS

TECHNOLOGY / LEADERSHIP

115 Linda Vista
Sedona, AZ 86336 USA
https://www.TechnicsPub.com

Edited by Sadie Hoberman
Cover design by Lorena Molinari

First Printing 2023

Copyright © 2023 by Mark Atkins and Terry Smith

ISBN, print ed.   9781634621816
ISBN, Kindle ed. 9781634621823
ISBN, ePub ed.   9781634621830
ISBN, PDF ed.   9781634621885

Library of Congress Control Number: 2022949762

*In loving memory of John Schutz,
who left us too soon, and
to whom we owe so much.*

Contents

Acknowledgments

"Now it's time to redefine myself." —Sean Carey, *Redefine*

This book is the culmination of our combined sixty-something years of experience, a period in which we have had to redefine ourselves many times. Our ability to reflect personally on our experiences and to reset and reinvent is, in many ways, due to the excellent advice and mentoring offered by leaders whom we have had the pleasure to work with. We thank them, especially Linda Bronstein, Nick Johantgen and Thana Velummylum, who gave us opportunities to embark with them on exciting new ventures, and Glen Carlson, who has been encouraging us to finish this book since the first draft in 2019—we're finally ready to give it wings! We'd also like to acknowledge the opportunities given to us by Geetha Velummylum and Kerrin Patterson to prove, and improve, our methodology—thank you.

This book would not have been possible without the encouragement of our colleagues: Frank Neumann and Kate Koch for helping us understand their challenges, John Steinbeck and Howard Diesel for openly supporting and promoting us, and Graham Witt for the many conversations on language; our friends, Vicky and James Donnelly for supporting us lovingly and with copious volumes of good food, music and wine; and our family, especially John

Atkins for his enthusiastic and detailed feedback. Also, a special thank you to Francesca Messori and Naomi Crain for their many years of creative support, hard work, and honest feedback.

Finally, a big thank you to Steve Hoberman and everyone at Technics Publications for bringing this book to life.

Foreword

A number of years ago, as CFO of a large Telecommunications company, I realised the potential value of better data management and established a Chief Data Office.

With the powers of computing today and of course artificial intelligence, data management is even more important – in fact essential for business success.

Governance and control of information is essential. We spoke often about a single source of truth and how essential that is. Good decisions will only come from that single source of truth. With that, of course is the need for a single understandable language so everyone is on the same page.

Business must drive the solutions to good data governance. Conversion of data to business information will drive the right solutions and minimise risk. The authors of this book have been on this journey for a long time and have learnt from many experiences.

This book will certainly help those on the journey to make better informed lower risk decisions.

I recommend it to you.

John Stanhope AM, chair of Port of Melbourne and chair of Bionics Institute

Introduction

Imagine a home where every room focuses on obtaining and eating food. And imagine that the food would provide no evidence of having "gone off" —no bad smells, no visible mold, nothing—so you don't know if consuming it will make you sick.

Due to the lack of expiry dates and diet suitability, the family members bring in and consume what they want and never dispose of leftovers, instead putting them into containers on a shelf in the room where they are consuming their meals. Eventually, there would be containers of food everywhere. Can you imagine the mess? Some of it remains edible, but most would be potentially poisonous. Some family members just get more food, and others just continually eat from their own stash.

---

[1] William Bruce Cameron, *Informal Sociology: A Casual Introduction to Sociological Thinking, Random House,* 1963.

That home is like many organizations in which we've worked. The rooms are their departments. The family is their team. The shelves are their network storage. And the food is their data (raw ingredients) and information (prepared dishes). That information is what *should* satiate their leaders' hunger without feelings of anxiety.

The good news is that it is relatively easy to achieve peace of mind around the information you consume so that you can lead with confidence.

This book presents a proven and award-winning framework of tools and techniques based on over 60 years of experience from the authors. This book will assist you with managing organizational knowledge without costly technology, reducing the risk of:

- regulatory non-compliance,
- ineffective *infotech* (information technology) spend,
- loss of organizational knowledge due to staff attrition, and
- unreliable information.

Over the next four chapters, we provide you with our four-point KSIR strategy—an antidote for risk:

(K)   Chapter 1, *Knowledge*—shows that the language of your organization is important. We illustrate through case studies how costly mistakes are being made because of ambiguous terminology and definitions. We then present a method for writing definitions that, through workshops, builds consensus while sharing knowledge between functional areas of the organization. This leads to more effective communication and, in turn, better-defined infotech requirements.

(S)   Chapter 2, *Sociality*—builds on the knowledge workshops to establish communities of practice that appreciate the importance of good information management. We discuss elements of change management and provide examples of how cultural behavior affects organizations, both positively and negatively. We discuss how knowledge and information management must shift back into the business community, supported by a no-blame, transparent leadership.

(I)   Chapter 3, *Infotech*—introduces a few of the many data-related topics. We look at data models, data warehouses, data management, etc., and propose the reason why information management needs to be a business-driven complement to the data management practices under the *information technology group* (IT). We introduce a proven methodology for improving information quality and how poor quality is, more often than not, due to broken business processes.
We also look at the amount of investment being made in infotech and the large number of failures

that are the result of that ineffective investment. And we explain how business language can be used as a method to improve communication between business and IT, thereby improving the success rate of infotech projects.

(R) Chapter 4, *Resources*—expands on information management as a business function introduced in earlier chapters. With a focus on managing artifacts, we discuss artifact curation and governance. We also introduce the concept of an organizational *business encyclopedia* that facilitates the KSIR methods by combining artifacts with the knowledge captured in definitions, enabling the management of business issues that are aligned with business strategy. This becomes the vessel for supporting and measuring the performance of your organization's information management community.

We reinforce these four points with case studies, and each chapter concludes with a positive example.

While the four-point KSIR strategy is the foundation for developing an effective knowledge and information management ecosystem, to be successful, the ecosystem must align these points by establishing business information management based on four *abilities*:

- *Accountability*—boundaries of roles, responsibilities, and rewards;
- *Visibility*—transparent acknowledgment, resolution, and monitoring of information-related issues;
- *Capability*—through awareness, training, and appropriate technologies; and
- *Measurability*—effective measures to enable progress reporting to support continuous improvement across the four points.

Establishing these abilities across all four points of the KSIR strategy delivers solid business assurance for senior managers and practical access to details about valuable business information and knowledge for all staff. And executing the KSIR strategy can begin in a single department and grow organically, or it can be part of a larger organizational change.

About the authors

Terry's personal story

I grew up in the United States in a large family (six kids). My parents couldn't afford much, especially college. If you were male, the military, police force, or some other blue-collar job was waiting for you. If you were female, your path was to graduate high school, get married, and have kids. I never did like that path.

I loved school; yes, I was a nerd. Not a genius, but definitely a nerd. I excelled in both math and English, thanks to my fear of the nuns who taught us. Eventually, I went to college—the first in my family of over thirty cousins. The challenge was what to choose. Although I loved English, I'll admit I was influenced by money; I did not want to struggle like my parents. I didn't think English careers were very lucrative (unless you became a famous writer), so I chose business. I loved numbers, so finance and accounting for me. Who wouldn't love working with spreadsheets!

After graduating, I became a financial analyst in the risk management department of a health insurance company. Although I was an accountant, my role had little to do with accounting and more with hunting for information. This was before the days of data warehousing and self-service reporting environments. When you asked IT to add one column to an existing report, they would charge $100,000 and take six months. Although the price tag was high, the timing was the killer. By the time I received the report, the question I was trying to answer would be superseded by ten more. Still sounds a bit familiar, doesn't it? I kept thinking, "it shouldn't be this hard."

So, I made friends with a colleague in IT who handed me a SAS programming manual and set up some JCL (I hadn't a clue what that was), and then said, "start programming girl!" (Back then, it was politically acceptable to call someone "girl.") I thought, how hard could it be! Well, the end result was that I had become the ultimate hunter-gatherer. My career in data science began way before data science became a buzzword.

Those combined skills led me into the world of consulting. I went from financial analyst to data warehouse consultant. I was multilingual; I was a business person who could speak tech talk. I've played in both fields, which gave me an interesting perspective of the "other" team. Some would call it the dark side—I'll let you choose which side is the dark side.

My favorite part of my consulting career was solving problems. I love a good puzzle. I remember a client who could not get their reporting system to reconcile with their billing system. They said it was impossible. Mark and I (having just started working together here in Australia) spent the weekend determined to solve that mystery and by Monday morning, found the missing pieces—and it balanced—audit issue resolved. The shocked look on their faces was priceless.

From consulting to business information management leader to business owner.

Now I spend my time educating the business world on language. I teach business people how to write clear definitions. That may sound strange, but my 30+ years of experience led to one major discovery: most information issues result from poor definitions, not defective systems. Align your language, and you'll get "the real" information. Only then can you make the best decisions.

Mark's personal story

I've always been a little obsessed with finding out how things work and making them efficient. My earliest memory of this was when I was about 11 years old. We had one of those tube-shaped vacuum cleaners, and as part of my chores, I had to clean and vacuum my room. One day, when I was cleaning my room after school, the vacuum cleaner started to make a different noise. It had never been very effective at picking up the dust from the rugs, so I decided to investigate.

When my mother came home from work, she discovered me in my bedroom sitting on the floor with the vacuum cleaner in pieces. She freaked out! But I found the problem (a misshapen impeller), which I repaired, and reassembled the machine. It worked much better after that, to the surprise of my mother.

As a teenager, I didn't have access to the high school computer (yes, one computer), which was reserved for students in another class. While working in the auto retail industry as a store manager during my twenties, I bought one of the first micro-computers—a Sinclair ZX81.[2] Some of my friends were earning a good salary as data-entry clerks, and I wanted to learn programming. I quickly outgrew its capability, having tried to write an inventory management system! But that experience was the key to my best example of creating efficiency.

When I was working as a process technician for a large petrochemical company, I was monitoring a chemical reactor in the early morning hours, and the process control computer failed to detect the end of the reaction. This frustrated me as I was eager to finish the batch and get the next one started before shift handover. None of the other operators seemed to care—less work for them! So, I went into the computer room, figured out from the manuals how to print out the program in question, and duly identified the bug, which I corrected with a red pen and marked it for the attention of the applications engineer.

Needless to say, this raised the attention of the plant management! To cut a long story short, I was engaged in another project to see if I could improve the process, which

---

[2] In the USA, the ZX81 was branded as the Timex Sinclair 1000.

I did by reducing the batch-cycle time by 45%. This led to three things: a reduction in manpower (I programmed myself out of a job); an angry union; and a staff position in the applications engineering department.

Today my focus is improving business performance and this book provides the essence of how I do that for the benefit of individuals in their organizations and, I hope, beyond!

CHAPTER 1

Knowledge

"The beginning of wisdom is the definition of terms."[3]

Organizational knowledge dilutes across the business: each time an employee leaves, changes role, or is absent for an extended period; when a function is outsourced; and during acquisitions and mergers. That loss of knowledge exacerbates an existing problem: our inability to clearly define business needs for infotech, which is a root cause of project failures, poor or conflicting data, and the high risk of regulatory non-compliance.

Knowledge is the first point of our strategy, being the foundation of all business endeavors, but how can we be certain our knowledge is correct? It stands to reason, therefore, that any knowledge on which decisions are made should be tested and validated or, at least, questioned. This

---

[3] This is incorrectly associated with Socrates:
https://philosophy.stackexchange.com/questions/45154/the-beginning-of-wisdom-is-the-definition-of-terms-socrates.

requires a well-structured approach toward organizational discourse.

Knowledge is either know what (explicit knowledge that can be written down) or know how (tacit knowledge that is attained from experience).

This chapter will focus on an organization's ability to capture and use knowledge of the *know what*, specifically the definition of basic everyday business concepts that are the foundation of our communication within the organization. These business concepts are so often misunderstood. (Chapter 4, *Resources*, will expand the *know what* to include important information artifacts, such as policies and procedures, dashboards, and more.)

If you think trying to capture an organization's knowledge about the concepts that they use to communicate is a waste of time, consider a statement that we use often—it's a shortened version of a quote attributed to Alan Greenspan:

"What you think I said is not what I think you heard!"[4]

---

[4] *Business Couples Secret Source,* Terry Smith and Mark Atkins, https://www.iheart.com/podcast/269-business-couples-secret-sa-71559305/episode/terry-smith-mark-atkins--74247966/.

Now consider the number of times you may have:

1. been arguing a point with someone for some time before realizing that you are in violent agreement; or

2. been part of an email chain where the author or main recipient is obviously misunderstanding the request; or

3. asked via an email for some information, to then receive a copy of the same request being forwarded to someone else, paraphrasing your request in a way that changes the request completely; or

4. … we could go on.

The case studies in this chapter will provide examples where situations of misunderstandings or misaligned terminology have directly impacted project success. We will give examples where ambiguity has been measured as a cost to projects, sometimes equating to many thousands of dollars.

You may not be aware of these kinds of situations affecting your organization because, frankly, some of the organizations in which we've worked have swept them under the carpet due to a cultural indisposition to make them known (we'll look at cultural behavior in Chapter 2, *Sociality*).

The objective of this chapter is to enable you to implement the core of our award-winning methodology: establishing the ability to align organizational knowledge through the clear definition of business terminology using a unique structured approach, and to capture that knowledge in an accessible and business-managed glossary. (In the last chapter, we'll show you how to expand that business glossary into a business encyclopedia.)

But first, we will provide a summary of our experiences and observations that led us to develop the KSIR principles and methods. We will then look at the underlying problem of why unmanaged business language costs money, and how it affects an organization's ability to get the information it needs to operate and compete.

Research—The cost of project failures

Projects fail for many reasons, and published statistics on project failures vary enormously, as do the reasons for those failures. According to various sources, failure rates range anywhere from 11% to 70%. That is an extremely wide range, so let's look at a few statistics. We all love numbers, don't we?

We have chosen stats from the Project Management Institute (PMI). PMI has been around since 1969 and is considered a leading professional association for project management professionals, with over 650,000 members worldwide.

According to PMI's *Pulse of the Profession* (2021), 12% of IT projects fail.[5] However, that number represents what was considered a "total" failure. Total failure is defined as:

- not meeting business objective(s),
- exceeding project budget, and
- not meeting the project deadline.

Of the *remaining* projects that didn't fail totally:

- 27% didn't meet their goals,
- 38% exceeded their initial budgets, and
- 45% were late.

It may be difficult to draw any conclusions from these stats, as so many variables impact a project's success. Still, if we focus on all projects that didn't meet their business objectives, approximately 36% of projects fail.

These statistics haven't changed much in the last decade and are most likely understated, as many political pressures will deem a project successful regardless of the outcome.

---

[5] Project Management Institute (2021), *Pulse of the Profession® - Beyond Agility Appendix - Section 6*, https://www.pmi.org/-/media/pmi/documents/public/pdf/learning/thought-leadership/pulse/pmi-pulse-2021-appendix.pdf.

Why do so many projects continue to fail? PMI 2021 statistics state many reasons (top 10 shown below):

1. Change in organization's priorities (41%)
2. Poor requirements gathering (40%)
3. Change in project objectives (38%)
4. Poor upfront planning (33%)
5. Inadequate/poor communication (28%)
6. Inadequate vision/goal (28%)
7. Ineffective risk management (27%)
8. Inadequate sponsor support (25%)
9. Poor change management (24%)
10. Poorly management dependencies (23%)

A survey conducted by PMI (2020), which included project professionals, project management office (PMO) directors and senior executives, revealed that 29% of projects were deemed failures.[6] (No information was provided regarding their criteria for success.)

Another research study by the Newton Group and Robert Walters Consulting found that 38% of failed projects were

---

[6] Project Management Institute (2020), *Pulse of the Profession® - Ahead of the Curve: Forging a Future-Focused Culture, Appendix - Section 2,* https://www.pmi.org/-/media/pmi/documents/public/pdf/learning/thought-leadership/pulse/pmi-pulse-2020-appendix.pdf.

caused by the inability to define information clearly, and 34% were focused on the solution rather than requirements.

Our experience has shown that undefined requirements, ambiguous definitions, and inadequate communication are at the root of the problem.

What is all this costing organizations? Again, let's look at PMI stats:

- In 2018—9.9% wasted for every dollar spent. This wastage varied by region, with China being the top performer at 7.6% wastage; US in the middle with 10.2%; and Australia hitting the highest wastage at 13.9%.
- In 2019—12% wasted.
- In 2020—11.4% wasted.
- In 2021—9.4% wasted.

Interestingly, according to PMI, the overall failure rate has decreased slightly during the pandemic, as well as the investment wastage; but the explanation for the improvement was that many of the planned projects were put on hold during the pandemic, particularly the larger more strategic projects—ones that generally have a far higher failure rate.

We've seen large investments in big data and analytics in recent years. Investment in artificial intelligence (AI) and business analytics was expected to hit over $274 billion in 2022.[7] It is these types of projects that are most impacted by poor definitions. Imagine saving just 10% of that figure— that's $27 billion. How much is 10% of your investment budget for AI and business analytics?

Most organizations struggle to bridge the gap between strategy and its practical implementation. Disruptive technologies like AI and machine learning are only as smart as the people behind them. If you want the job done right, your people need more than just talent—they need the right training and the right processes.

The semantic gap

Infotech projects continue to fail.

One of the underlying reasons is due to what's called *the semantic gap*. This is the difference between the ambiguity of descriptions for objects in the real world using natural languages and the ability to translate these into computational representations within highly structured programming languages and, therefore, data.

---

[7] Actual 2022 investment not known at the time of writing.

Case study: What is a student?

As humans, we can often observe problems caused by the semantic gap after the fact. For example, a university had undersubscribed their student intake due to a misunderstanding over the data used to determine the "number of students." They included in the count applicants who had been offered admission to the university (a place) but had not accepted. This caused a loss in target revenue of approximately 15%. The issue was resolved to prevent such misunderstandings in the future by ensuring that all stakeholders agreed to an understanding of the student life cycle and the use of appropriately qualified terminology when communicating with the data and analytics group, for example, "applicant" versus "admitted student" versus "enrolled student".

Yet, as organizations attempt to respond faster and faster to demands for more data and more digital capability, the emphasis appears to have shifted from improving design methodologies that attempt to minimize the semantic gap, to promises of technological advances that attempt to resolve those demands through data science and, more specifically, artificial intelligence (AI).

We have no doubt that the tables will turn again, and new design methodologies will bring data and enterprise architecture, and new design methodologies, back into vogue. In fact, as we write this, a recent alternative to the data warehouse architectures (data mesh) is being declared as both a valid approach and dead by the data architecture profession! (We look at data warehouse and software development methodologies in Chapter 3, *Infotech*, under

Data Models and *Software Development Methodologies,* respectively.)

As an example of how well new technologies perform, in 2018, Gartner predicted that through 2022, 85 percent of AI projects would fail to deliver, and recent reports (at the time of writing in 2022) are saying that failure rates are even higher.[8]

Computers at their heart are very simple—it's the programming that has become complex, with AI incorporating the contextual references and biases of the programmer and the data sets used to train the algorithms. But ignoring AI for the moment, most organizations still rely on some form of business intelligence to provide the information they need to operate and compete.

Organizations are being misled by the "data-driven" mantra in the belief that data alone will allow them to compete successfully. You will no doubt have been told the merits of *Agile development, DevOps,* and *rapid application development (RAD).*[9] Each of these are attempts to make software development faster through incrementally

---

[8] https://www.gartner.com/en/newsroom/press-releases/2018-02-13-gartner-says-nearly-half-of-cios-are-planning-to-deploy-artificial-intelligence.

[9] We discuss these in more detail in the *Software Development Methodologies* section in Chapter 3, *Infotech.*

releasing versions of the software and with more engagement of the business stakeholders. Although they all have merits, the downside is that these methods shortcut critical thinking—both in business and IT—that underpins successful infotech investment.

In IT, this *fail fast* philosophy is, in many cases, leading to a decline in the number of information designers, such as data modelers, data architects, and information architects, because they are seen as a bottleneck in the development process. The number of infotech project failures clearly show that this approach is not fiscally sound.

These approaches sound good in theory, but as a professor of ours once said, "in theory, there is no difference between practice and theory!" In practice, good *design* cannot be done incrementally—at least not in the traditional way—which leads to eliminating the design roles mentioned above.

In response, we have seen two behavioral shifts from these approaches to infotech projects, both driven by the good intentions of the people involved: the architectural design activity is partially absorbed by the business analysts, who are trained to be skilled in describing requirements, *not* in architectural design; and the data design is absorbed by the developers, who are trained and skilled in process automation, also *not* in architectural design. Research has shown that the descriptive and design processes require very different skill sets.[10] As a result, there are an increasing number of people trying to be a *jack of all trades*, who are building solutions that are highly likely to fail.

The overall effect must be recognized as lost organizational knowledge that potentially puts the organization at a disadvantage in the longer term.

Closing the semantic gap

Programming languages are highly structured. They require input statements that conform to well-specified:

- *syntax*—the order in which individual words and symbols can be presented (in statements and expressions); and

- *semantics*—the precise meaning of the words and symbols (functions, operators, constants, and variables) in the statements and expressions.

Sentences in natural languages are also structured, despite being referred to as semi-structured or unstructured in the data world. But the syntax, being grammar, can vary while still intending to convey the same meaning. And semantics,

---

[10] Graeme Simsion, *Data Modeling: Theory and Practice*, Technics Publications, 2007.

being the meaning of individual words, can vary vastly according to context, pronunciation, and spelling. All of this introduces ambiguity in spoken and written language. (We look at types and examples of ambiguity later in this chapter.)

Software development methodologies have tried over the years to address the semantic gap using diagrammatic and formally structured ways of presenting statements of fact to the programmer, or even generating computer code directly from those statements. However, they are still dependent on clear definitions of the things about which the statements are being made.

So, why not put some more rigid constraints on the way business concepts are described using natural language as a means of identifying ambiguity and reducing it in order to communicate more clearly—not just to software developers, but to our colleagues as well?

Methods of logically expressing and testing natural language sentences have existed since the nineteenth century! (See *Sentence Diagramming* later in this chapter.)

We will shortly explore types of ambiguity and then introduce our method of writing business definitions. This method not only reduces ambiguity but also:

- builds collaboration and establishes ownership of the organization's terminology;

- is compatible with Agile development;
- captures organizational knowledge;
- improves communication; and
- reduces the risk of project failure.

To illustrate how ambiguity can cause project failure, we want to share a spectacular example of how misunderstood terminology led to a $200,000+ project failure.

Case study: Ambiguity causes project failure

An insurance company had started its digital conversion journey and needed to send policies to its customers electronically. The systems had already been modified to generate the policies and then transfer them to a third-party email service provider. The part of the project we're referring to, the reporting component, needed to measure the time taken between the policy being produced, the time it was received by the third-party, and the time it was received by the customer.

The project had two objectives: regulation and compliance. Consumer law requires that a customer receive a policy within a certain number of days. The insurance company needed to know if the electronic delivery failed so that a printed copy could be sent in time to fulfill their regulatory obligation. The second objective was to measure the compliance of the third-party to their service level agreement, which stated that they would perform the policy delivery service within a certain timeframe, providing dates and times of attempts to deliver an email.

At the time, we provided management services to the insurance company to backfill an empty position due to a short-term secondment. We were called in to an emergency project meeting. During the user acceptance testing, it transpired that the business stakeholder said that the reporting dashboard didn't look right. But the development team was adamant that they had applied the user requirements exactly and that the data must be wrong.

So, the third-party was summoned to this meeting along with the business stakeholders, the project managers, a developer from the operational system, a developer from the third-party, the developers of the reporting system, the business analyst, and us, as representatives for the business intelligence (BI) design manager. They were all crowded around the meeting table and started to talk about their various understandings of the problem. It soon became obvious to us that there was confusion due to a misunderstanding over the terminology used for the part of the process, where the email was sent to the customer. We mapped out the process on the whiteboard and clarified the labels at each step of the process, along with the date and time data captured at each step.

Our background in system design was useful in envisaging the various points in time and confirming them with the developers. These points in time were:

1. A policy is generated.
2. A regular process combines (batches) any policies that are waiting to be sent.
3. A connection is established between the policy system and the third-party.
4. The batch file is sent.
5. The batch receipt is confirmed to the policy system.
6. The batch receipt time is recorded by the third-party.
7. The third-party emails each policy and the time is reported.
8. If an email failure occurs, for example, due to the customer's mailbox being full (a soft error) or the email address is invalid (a hard error), the failure is reported. In the case of the soft error, step 7 is repeated after waiting for a specified time. If the email send process (step 7) has failed three times, the

process is aborted, and the failure is reported.
Note: the absence of a failure does not indicate successful delivery.

9. The email is received by the customer.

It soon became evident that the same words were being used by different attendees of the meeting, with different interpretations of the words "email successfully sent." For the service level agreement monitoring, the business stakeholders had wanted to know how long each policy took from point 5 to point 9 and had assumed that the term "email successfully sent" meant the same as "email successfully received"! You can't blame the business stakeholder for not knowing the details of how an email process works. It turned out that several things had gone wrong in this project:

The definition of the term "email successfully sent" was not clarified with the business stakeholders. The time at point 5 was not being recorded by the policy system, so the service level measurement was reliant on the third-party's successful reporting of step 6. The business stakeholders did not realize that it is not always possible to know if an email is received. This is because some email systems will not report delivery success or failure for security and privacy reasons.

The first point here is that the reporting component could not provide the information to report on the service level agreement as wanted by the insurance company, but they could report based on their interpretation of the agreement. The second point is this: if the terminology had been properly defined and confirmed, it would have been realized that the compliance requirements would not have been met with confidence by this email delivery design, and an alternative process could have been sought.

Ambiguity

Words can mean different things to different people at different times. Using the wrong word can cause needless arguments; using a less specific word can cause ambiguity, which leads to assumptions. And we all know that the least questioned assumptions are often the most questionable.

So, what exactly is ambiguity? Simply put, ambiguity is inexactness. It occurs when a word, phrase, or entire sentence is open to multiple interpretations. This occurs quite easily in any language, but particularly in natural language, such as English.

Ambiguity can be a useful tool in writing, particularly in creative writing, in poetry, or song writing; it can allow the reader (or listener) to draw their own conclusions. It also works well in disguising insults and sarcasm, although we would never engage in such tactics! But ambiguity in the business world can cause all kinds of problems and cost a considerable amount of money.

There are different types of ambiguity. The focus of our method is reducing *lexical ambiguity* and *syntactic ambiguity*, although we will also describe *textual ambiguity*.

Lexical ambiguity

Lexical ambiguity, also known as semantic ambiguity, occurs in a sentence because of *word choice*—a single word can mean different things to different people. Of the most common 9,000 words in the English language, 64% have more than one meaning; this increases to 95% for the most frequently used 3,000 words.[11]

This is an increasing challenge as our workforce today becomes more diverse. Different cultures and different generations can have very different meanings for the same word. Much in the same way that certain behaviors can be perceived differently across cultures, for example, direct eye contact in some cultures can represent active listening and respect, while in others, it is perceived as a form of intimidation.

Lexical ambiguity does not occur just across cultures; it is very prevalent within a given culture—the culture within an organization. And it occurs in both verbal and written communication. In verbal communications, mistaken words are much more easily recognized, as there are visual clues to judge the reactions to our dialogue, assuming one is paying attention.

---

[11] Meral Ozturk, *Multiple Meanings in the EFL Lexicon,* International Journal of Curriculum and Instruction, v9 n2 p1-10 2017, https://eric.ed.gov/?id=EJ1207245.

Whereas, with written language, one can never be absolutely sure how the reader will interpret the message being conveyed. The best we can do is: 1) increase our vocabulary so that our choice of words is thoroughly considered in our written communication, and 2) understand how the arrangement of words (syntax) affects how our message may be received.

The English language, as with any language, is a complex system of syntax and, in many languages, *morphology*.[12]

We are all guilty of taking simple words used in everyday business for granted. We *assume* everyone we communicate with has the same perception of a given word, especially in the work environment. "Customer" is the perfect example. How many different interpretations (or views) of "customer" does your organization have? Take a poll and ask, "*How many customers do we have?*" You may be surprised how many different answers you'll get.

Each functional area of an organization will have a different view. Marketing may include anyone who is a current customer as well as any potential customers. Sales may count anyone who has agreed to or signed a purchase order. Finance may include only those who pay the invoices or

---

[12] Morphology is how words are formed and relate, for example, in English when we change the suffix of verbs to indicate tense or add an "s" to change nouns from singular to plural.

hold an account. Customer service may include anyone who calls with a query or complaint. Product development may include anyone who *uses* a product or service. All of these scenarios will result in a different count of customers. And all may be correct given their context.

Case study: What is a customer?

We ran some workshops for a large bank whose strategic objective was to become more customer-focused. Before we could even determine what that meant or how we could measure it, we asked each participant to write on a post-it note the number of customers the bank had. There were 24 participants, mostly managers and department heads. We received 18 different answers, ranging from 3.5 million to over 50 million. They obviously had different definitions for "customer."

Syntactic ambiguity

Syntactic ambiguity, sometimes referred to as structural ambiguity, is about the *arrangement (or sequence) of the words in the sentence.* It occurs when the whole sentence or part of a sentence can have multiple interpretations.

This type of ambiguity may often lead to humorous results (although not in the workplace), for example:

- *"Let's stop <u>controlling</u> people."*

Should we stop controlling other people, or should we stop people who are controlling others?

- *"Visiting relatives can be exhausting."*

What's exhausting; the relatives when they visit us, or when we visit them? Who's doing the visiting?

- *"The professor said on Monday he would give an exam."*

Did he *say it* on Monday or is he *giving the exam* on Monday?

- *"The cat chased the mouse until it stumbled and fell."*

Who (or what) is *it*? Did the cat stumble and fall, or did the mouse stumble and fall?

- *"You should bring wine or beer and dessert."*

Should I bring wine and dessert, should I bring beer and dessert, or should I just bring wine? I should probably bring all three, just to be safe!

In these examples, we can see how tricky some *parts of speech*[13] can be. What appears to be a verb may actually be functioning as an adjective (controlling and visiting). The

---

[13] part of speech—a category to which a word is assigned in accordance with its syntactic functions. In English the main parts of speech are noun, pronoun, adjective, determiner, verb, adverb, preposition, conjunction, and interjection. [Source: Oxford English Dictionary]

placement of a *prepositional phrase*[14] (on Monday) can completely change how we interpret something. Pronouns can lead to all kinds of misinterpretations; what exactly does 'it' stand for? And those conjunctions—when is 'and' and 'or' really an 'and/or' situation? (The missing oxford comma has cost some organizations millions.)

Understanding grammar plays a critical part in writing a well-formed, unambiguous sentence. Grammar is the system and structure of language. Yes, our language has structure. Although not all of us apply that structure. Applying good grammar is the first step in making our communication clear and unambiguous.

Textual ambiguity

Textual ambiguityoften occurs because of unfamiliarity of the language or insufficient context. An example of textual ambiguity, and the cause of much confusion in the work environment, is the use of abbreviations, or what most organizations refer to as *acronyms*.[15] One of our clients had

---

[14] A prepositional phrase is a short phrase that contains a noun preceded by a preposition (a short word like "in", "of", "on", "after") that describes the relation between the noun and another word in the sentence.

[15] An acronym is a type of abbreviation, one that can be pronounced as a word.

so many abbreviations (585) in use that a new hire was lucky to understand half of what was said, particularly in meetings where it can be quite intimidating to keep interrupting the speaker to ask what the acronym means. But believe us, half of the attendees couldn't tell you what many of the acronyms meant.

When we're reading a definition, it's the language we use that will convey the meaning. Unfortunately, people reading the definition (or any communication) may not have English as their first language or may not have an industry background, which is too often assumed.

We know organizations operate in functional units. Each of these areas operates their own processes and systems, develops their own distinct language, and defines things within their own context. This leads to the existence of the same terms with different meanings, as well as different meanings for the same term.

But there is terminology that requires agreement across functional areas—our core terms and particularly our key metrics. We have often heard the argument, "It's just too hard!" But our method will help you achieve consensus.

The first step in gaining consensus is removing the ambiguity. It's easier to get agreement if definitions are written in a structured format, thereby creating alignment. If everyone knows those definitions, it enables understanding and better communication.

If those definitions are stored in a business glossary that everyone has access to, there are so many more benefits:

- it increases efficiency—staff do not have to spend time redefining for every project, therefore, improves productivity and provides more time for innovation;
- it provides easy access to knowledge which reduces risk;
- it advocates ownership and accountability which establishes trust; and
- it improves our ability to make better decisions.

One thing that must be understood about a business glossary is that it is not a "data dictionary." Instead, building a glossary is about building a community.

If we don't do the definition management, we are just creating another glossary to add to the many that already exist. We can't create alignment without creating the community, and we don't get the benefits unless those definitions are accessible, accepted, managed, and their reuse is measured.

Case study—Make the intangible tangible: measure project time spent on definitions.

We spent some time as stand-in data managers for a national insurance company in Australia that had a project to develop a customer-sentiment executive dashboard. The marketing department had already engaged a third party to conduct market surveys of any insurance company customers that had recently made a claim or had some other interaction. The customer management department had established the data feeds with the third party. These included the customer data and the corresponding questionnaire results data. (However, these were established without any data management involvement in specifying the data structures and questionnaire versioning—but those issues are for another story.)

One of the dimensions to display on the dashboard was brand—this insurance company had many brands under which it sold personal insurance. The development team raised a concern that several tables in the data warehouse contained brand information and needed to determine which was the "correct" source. We decided to measure the amount of effort involved just in the meetings called to discuss and attempt to resolve the issue (so not including any research work that the analysts performed prior to meeting).

In the meantime, we produced a structured definition for "brand," which we then discussed, edited, and obtained agreement with each of the seven brand managers.

Using the standard person-hour rate at that time, we calculated the following costs.

- Project meetings:
  2 hours x 8 people (not including ourselves) x $1000
  = $16,000

- Defining brand: Initial definition effort, including research,
  3 hours + (7 x 0.5 hours brand manager meetings) x $1000
  = $6,500

There are also other important points to make about the knowledge gained:

- During the discussions with the brand managers, who provided the actual brand names (values for the dashboard dimension), we discovered that they were involved in a major rebranding exercise.

- None of the brand managers were aware of the dashboard project and its inclusion of brand data.

- None of the several sources of brand in the data warehouse had the correct set of brand names that was agreed in the definition (each of these sources had been created to support past projects, a classic example of creating new rather than fixing the existing).

Yet our observation is that nearly every reporting project spends time finding data to fit business terms, rather than defining and verifying that definition once for reuse.

In this example, assuming three projects during the course of a year need to provide "brand" data, and assuming that the first project needs to include a one-hour definition workshop with all eight team members, plus seven subject matter experts and a skilled facilitator, we can calculate the total cost and savings as:

- Cost to first project:
  1 hour x 16 people x $1000
  = $16,000

- Savings for the year:
  meetings for 2 other projects x $16,000
  = $32,000

That is a pretty good return on investment.

One of the reasons we developed our definition writing method was our experience working in multi-generational and multi-cultural organizations, where we noticed a couple of things: how those whose first language is not English and are not fluent in English will often not conjugate verbs, using instead the base form of the verb; and how those same people will use simple sentence structures. Yet communication is still generally effective, regardless of the verb form, as long as the terms are well understood.

Let's have a look at a situation where culture and language affected operations and almost caused disastrous results due to a misunderstanding of a term. Everyone knows the difference between a child and a woman, right? Apparently not, as this case study on TUI Airways shows.

Case study: Definition of "child" [16]

Picture this: Pilots of a TUI Airways Boeing 737-800, waiting to depart from Birmingham, UK to Palma de Mallorca, review their load sheet, which estimates how heavy the plane is, given the number of adult and child passengers, and the amount of luggage assumed for each.

This load sheet guides how much speed the pilots need when taking off. Get it wrong and lives are at risk.

---

[16] David Kaminski-Morrow, *TUI 737 weight incident traced to 'Miss' interpretation of female passengers,* 8 April 2021, https://www.flightglobal.com/safety/tui-737-weight-incident-traced-to-miss-interpretation-of-female-passengers/143223.article.

In this case, the load sheet data was wrong—more than 1.2 tonnes less than the actual aircraft weight and 1.6 tonnes less than the flight plan! While the pilots recognized discrepancies between the load sheet, which reported 65 instead of the expected 29 child passengers, they dismissed this, along with the baggage-weight discrepancies, as caused by pandemic-related travel disruptions.

Perhaps very luckily, they took off without incident because they employed a slightly higher thrust level than the load sheet data required.

While risk didn't turn into reality in this case, most of us would prefer not to have such close calls happening when we fly.

So, what went wrong?

TUI, a British-based airline, had instigated an upgrade of their reservation software during their pandemic flight suspension. They'd hired an overseas software developer to undertake the upgrade. This is not unusual and was probably a cost-conscious solution. But TUI did not undertake any language analysis and term definition work before engaging the software developers.

In TUI's case, this was a negligent and life-threatening move.

The country in which the upgrade was developed applied language in the manner that was accurate within their culture. They associated the titles "Ms" to adult women and "Miss" to children. You can see where we're going with this!

Everything looked fine. The upgrade tested fine, it was released, and as flight restrictions lifted, passengers used the system to book seats and check in with their luggage.

Although the error that adult passengers were being misclassified as children had later been found, two other flights were affected that day, and all because of a language difference in how the two cultures involved define the titles "Ms" and "Miss".

Business glossaries versus data dictionaries

In the previous case study, had TUI defined the business need to identify a child versus an adult and translated this need to the appropriate data, for example, using age instead of title, the situation could have been avoided. To explain this, we need to clarify the difference between business glossaries and data dictionaries.

Business glossaries have always been an important part of any organization's attempt to clarify its language and there are typically many glossaries in any sizeable organization. Many of these glossaries are developed in a given department (in isolation), usually for a specific project (maybe as part of a requirements document), or for a process or standard operating procedure. And we all know how aligned and consistent the definitions in these glossaries are likely to be!

There is now a growing emphasis on the importance of consolidating business terminology within a single glossary. Still, there is no emphasis on definition quality, nor is there a method of identifying the inconsistencies and aligning the language across the organization. Instead, the expectation is that it will magically be sorted out if it is all in one place.

On top of trying to consolidate those glossaries, organizations try to combine their business glossary with information about data (metadata), such as field names, data types, and brief descriptions. This metadata is typically extracted from data dictionaries, which of course are system specific. So, data with the same name may be found in multiple systems, each with a different definition or different values. Therefore, this metadata cannot be combined with business terms effectively.

Also, the business terminology and data are often not directly related. There is frequently a very complex relationship, and the approach of simply spelling out a data element and calling it a business term does not resolve that complexity. In fact, it gives a false perception of the real relationship to, and the meaning of, the business terminology. This is the semantic gap we previously talked about.

The structured definition

We would now like to introduce you to the Intralign[17] Definition Standard, which we developed to enable very clear definitions and a means to close or narrow that semantic gap.

At the heart of a good business glossary are well-written definitions. A good definition is both concise and

---

[17] Intralign is a registered trademark of Intraversed Pty Ltd in Australia.

unambiguous, providing as much information as possible with as few words as necessary. This, in turn, requires the writer to have a reasonable grasp of the language in use and access to appropriate tools, such as a dictionary, a thesaurus, and grammar references.

We will get into some grammar later in this section. This often causes some anxiety, particularly for those who were not formally taught grammar in school. Stick with us, it will be worth it in the end, and we will provide some good grammar references to use in everyday communications.

The Intralign definition standard is loosely based on Purdue University's online writing lab (OWL),[18] which states that there are three parts to a good definition:

1. the **term** being defined;
2. its **classification** — what it is; and
3. any **differentiating characteristics** that make this term different from other members of its class.

The above states *what* should be included in a definition, but it is left to the author to determine the *how*. And since there were no standards on writing business definitions, we have developed a standard and a methodology for writing clear business definitions.

---

[18] https://owl.purdue.edu/owl/general_writing/common_writing_assignments/definitions.html.

The objective of the Intralign Definition Standard is to provide a structured approach to writing the classification and the differentiating characteristics which encourage the author to construct the definition using simple phrases. Simple phrases allow business stakeholders to easily read, collaborate in the definition process, and confirm that individual phrases are correct.

Each statement (or phrase), which we call a *business rule,* is based on a simple sentence structure: *subject-verb-object,* where the subject is the term being defined and the object of each statement is another related business term. For example, let's define the term "student" in the context of a university. Being a simple term, everyone at the university should know what a student is. The Oxford English Dictionary tells us that a student is:

student | ˈstjuːd(ə)nt |

noun

a person who is studying at a university or other place of higher education: *a **student of** sociology* | *a maths student* | [as modifier]: *student loans.*

• a school pupil: *high-school students.*

• [*as modifier*] denoting someone who is studying in order to enter a particular profession: *a group of student nurses.*

• a person who takes an interest in a particular subject: *a **student of** the free market.*

They all work. What's the problem? Why should we bother? Earlier in this chapter, we included a case study about the trouble the lack of a definition of this simple term caused a university when they asked for a count of 'students', and how our methodology resolved the issue.

Most universities, if not all, have a student management system (sometimes more than one) used to capture information pertaining to: applications, admissions, enrolments, classes, timetables, and more. And because of this, these systems contain more than just students. These systems include applicants, students, alumni, lecturers, and more. Extracting data from these systems requires an understanding of the life cycle of a student and the rules that determine if the person in the system is indeed a "student".

With that in mind, a structured definition of a student might be:

student

is a **person**   (classification)

that must either be admitted to a **course of study**   (functional)

or enrolled in at least one **unit of study**   (functional)

Here we have provided the rules to identify if the person is indeed a student and have established the relationship of the student to a course of study and to one or more units of study, thereby, building our ontology.

> *An Ontology, our context being from computer science, is explained later in this chapter in the section* Ontologies and Knowledge Graphs. *An ontology is essentially a map of how objects, or information about those objects, relate to each other.*

Also, by knowing the term-to-term relationships, and recording them as part of the organization's business glossary, we can assess the impact that a change to one definition might have on its related terms' definitions.

The definition standard uses syntactical rules to add structure and consistency. The overall benefit is that each business rule can be read and verified independently by the stakeholders, which leads to quick and easy approval.

The classification rule

As per Purdue's OWL, we start with the term itself and a single classification rule. The classification establishes a taxonomy for business terminology. In the above example, our classification is "person". But not all classifications are that simple.

> *The common classifications that any organization will deal with are terms relating to "people", "organizations", "places", and "things". It's the* things *we deal with that can be tricky because we're not accustomed to articulating what something actually is.*

Too often we see people define something by where it is, what it's made up of, or when it happens, but find it difficult to express what something is. We forget to step back from our own preconceptions and that is why the first part of the structured definition has a very explicit structure, and will always use the verb 'is':

business term	is	**what**
[subject]	*[verb]*	*[object]*

Once we've determined what it is, we can expand on Purdue's differentiating characteristics in two ways:

1. by exposing the relationships between terms, thereby documenting the organization's ontology; and
2. by defining different statement types to further describe the differentiating characteristics.

The differentiating characteristics

Following the classification rule, we want to know the purpose of the term, which we write as one or more *functional rules*. These tell us why this term is important, why we have it, and what it does. If the term has no purpose (or consequence—see next paragraph), then we should question the need for a definition. Once we have determined the classification and the functional rule, based on the 80/20 rule we are 80% on our way to having a very good definition. Additional rule types add clarity but be aware of diminishing returns on effort.

Most of our terms will have a functional rule, but there are instances when the term we are defining doesn't have a function but instead will have a consequence. For example, a serious adverse reaction to a pharmaceutical product. Instead, we may have one or more *consequential rules* that state what must occur. This typically happens when we are defining something that is not under the organization's control, but instead is the result of some event or incident that the organization must react to or deal with.

Other rule types include:

- characteristic rules—to describe distinct features or properties;
- compositional rules—to identify its components or parts;
- formula rules—to define the calculation of metrics and measures;
- conditional rules—to declare if a preceding rule is based on some condition or constraint; and
- notational rules—to annotate the definition with additional information, such as examples.

Not all terms will use all the different rule types. But each term definition must have a classification and at least a functional and/or consequential rule.

All metrics and measures must also include formula rules. The functional and formula rules are the most important when defining a metric or measure. The functional rule for a metric tells us why we calculate this metric. That is, what does the metric tell us? This will also ensure that the metric is used appropriately.

The general structure

The general structure of a business rule is shown in *figure 1* and described in this section.

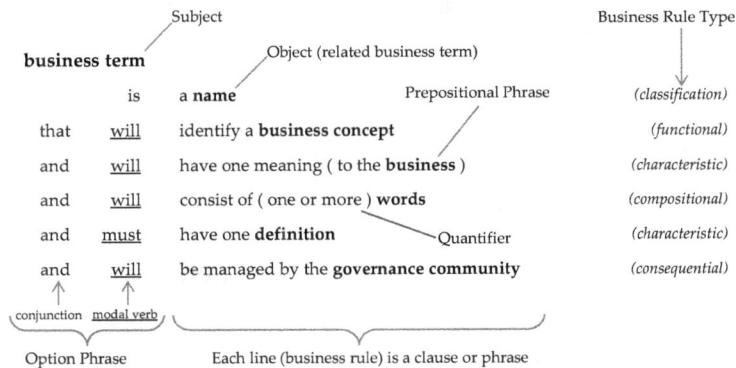

Figure 1—A structured definition for "business term"

The first business rule (as previously mentioned) is always the classification which will begin with the verb "is" and end with an object (the related term).

The second business rule (after the classification) is introduced with the relative pronoun "that" and will either be a function rule or a consequential rule.

The remaining business rules will commence with what we call an option phrase.

The option phrase includes the appropriate conjunction — "and", "or", "if", etc. — and one of six modal verbs — "must", "shall", "will", "should", "can", and "may".

The modal verb in the *option phrase* makes it possible to then use the base form of the verb in the main clause of the business rule (assuming that it is written using *active voice*, which is what we want). Using the base form of a verb is founded on our observation that it is easier for those who do not have English as a first language and often struggle with conjugation.

The option phrase is followed by a predicate clause that may contain a single prepositional phrase. Each predicate clause will end with a related business term.

The predicate clause can consist of a sequence containing single instances of each part of speech: *adverb, verb, adjective, noun.* It may also include a *quantifier* (see description below).

The prepositional phrase can consist of a sequence containing single instances of each part of speech: *preposition, adjective, noun*; and may also include a *quantifier*.

The following rules apply:

- The noun can be a compound noun (a noun containing two or more words), for example, "business concept", "governance community", and should also be a business term unless the predicate clause also contains a prepositional phrase. In this case the business term will be the object of the prepositional phrase.

- The quantifier determines whether the noun (or term) is plural, and can be: a determiner, for example, the articles "a", "an", or "the"; a pronoun, for example, "its", "our", "that", or "their"; or a short cardinal or ordinal phrase, for example, "one", "two", "at least three", "more than one", "first", "last", etc.

The general structure will work for most rule types. Here are two examples. Note how the second example, "part-time employee", will inherit the definition of the first through its classification rule.

employee	*(business term)*
is a **person**	*(classification)*
that is hired under an **employment contract**	*(consequential)*
to perform the specified duties of their **position**	*(functional)*
and will be entitled	*(characteristic)*
to the minimum **employee benefits**	
per the **National Employment Standards**	*(compound object)*

part-time employee	*(business term)*
is an **employee**	*(classification)*
that will work less than the total hours of a standard **workweek**	*(consequential)*
and will receive all **employee benefits** on a **pro-rata basis**	*(characteristic)*

Some rule types will differ slightly, such as conditional rules. Conditional rules are constructed as a set of rules and separated into multiple lines. The conditional rule will still begin with a conjunction, for example, "if" or "unless", but will not be followed by a modal verb. Instead, it will be followed by the subject of the condition followed by the condition, for example:

claimant	*(business term)*
is a **person**	*(classification)*
that will lodge a **claim**	*(functional)*
and may receive compensation for a **loss**	*(consequential)*
if the **loss**	*(conditional)*
is covered under the **insurance policy**	*(conditional)*

As well as reducing the risk of regulatory non-compliance, capturing clear definitions from key stakeholders in your organization has the additional benefit of helping to retain organizational knowledge that is otherwise diluted or lost through staff movement and attrition.

Sentence diagramming

In primary school, Terry was taught a technique called sentence diagramming, that was used to verify if a sentence was grammatically correct. Sentence diagramming is a visual representation of the structure of a sentence. In the diagram, each word in the sentence has a particular placement that highlights both the part of speech and the relationship the word has to other words in the sentence. Diagramming teaches how to look beyond the literary order of the sentence. It focuses on how words in the sentence function and how they relate to each other—the logical order. We can write a sentence in many ways, but if we can diagram it, then it will be logically and grammatically correct.

Sentence diagramming began in 1847 when Stephen Watkins Clark published the book, *A Practical Grammar: In Which Words, Phrases and Sentences are Classified According to Their Offices; and Their Various Relationships to One Another.*[19]

In his book, he described his "balloon" method, placing each word in a circle and arranging the circles according to

---

[19] S. W. Clark, A. M., *A Practical Grammar: In Which Words, Phrases, and Sentences are Classified According to Their Offices; and Their Various Relationships to One Another*, Fortieth Edition, Revised, A. S. Barnes & Co, 1868, https://ia600209.us.archive.org/10/items/ practicalgrammar00clar/practicalgrammar00clar.pdf.

function. It was a revolutionary method of teaching grammar, but it wasn't that easy to draw. The diagrams might look like a fleet of airships or a collection of hot-dog rolls.

This was followed in 1877 by Alonzo Reed and Brainerd Kellogg in their book, *Higher Lessons in English.*[20] The Reed-Kellogg method of diagramming sentences has evolved with English grammar over the decades and is still taught in some schools today.

A simple sentence, "The beginning of wisdom is the definition of terms." would look like this:

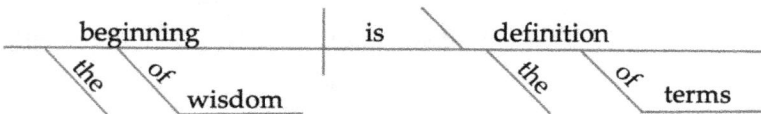

Figure 2 — Diagramming a simple sentence

A *simple* template, showing parts of speech, is shown in *Figure 3*.

---

[20] Alonzo Reed, A.M., and Brainerd Kellogg, A.M., Higher Lessons in English. A Work on English Grammar and Composition, in which the Science of the Language is made tributary to the Art of Expression. A Course of practical lessons carefully graded, and adapted to every day use in the school-room. Revised Edition, Effingham Maynard & Co., 1890, https://www.google.com.au/books/edition/English_Grammar_and_Composition/yqwyAQAAMAAJ.

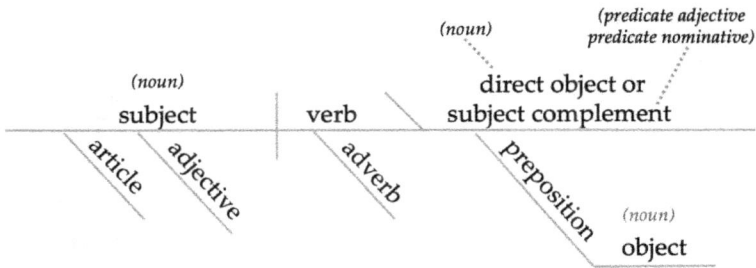

Figure 3—Sentence Diagramming Template

A sentence diagram shows the relationship between the words, phrases, and clauses, with the main part of the sentence (subject, verb, and object) on the horizontal line and all modifiers (articles, adjectives, adverbs, prepositional phrases, etc.) shown below the horizontal line attached to the word they qualify (or describe). They can become quite complex when dealing with long sentences.

This is the method Terry learned when grammar was still taught in schools. However, the first step was to circle the nouns and underline the verbs. This helped identify the main part of the sentence that would be placed on the horizontal line.

Diagramming was Terry's favorite part of grammar class, but it has become a lost art. She still believes it was the reason she became a data modeler. Notice the similarity with data modeling notation—circling the nouns (the entities) and underlining the verbs (the relationships).

> *We would recommend diagramming sentences to anyone teaching (or learning) grammar as it is much more visual and interactive. Some crazy people might even say it's fun!*

If you'd like to learn more about sentence diagramming, we recommend *Grammar Revolution*, by Elizabeth O'Brien.[21]

Ontologies and knowledge graphs

Earlier in this chapter, we introduced our structured definition writing standard, which captures explicit knowledge about business terminology in a way that creates an *ontology* of the organization.

While ontology is the philosophy of existence or being, in computer science an ontology is a model of one or more *domains of information*. It is used to represent the naming and definition of the domain's concepts and how those concepts are related. Within any organization, the concepts align with the terminology of the business and will either be concrete, such as plant and machinery in a water processing

---

[21] https://www.english-grammar-revolution.com/english-grammar-exercise.html.

company, or be abstract, such as the curriculum in an educational institute.

We know we're going to get a bit philosophical here (pun intended) but stay with us, and we promise you'll get where we're coming from.

Creating an ontology

Ontology as a philosophy is concerned with a system of *categories* for classifying *entities* –things that exist—either as *particulars*, such as apples and oranges, or universals, such as colors and shapes. The general list of categories is:

- *substances*—things that exist independently, such as apples and oranges;

- *properties*—things that collectively may describe an entity, being either categorical (what it is like) or dispositional (what it can do);

- *modality*—the concepts of possibility, actuality, and necessity;

- *relations*—the way things (the relata) are connected or positioned with each other in time and space;

- *states of affairs*—complex entities that are a combination of other entities that may be considered atomic, simply consisting of a particular and a property, such as the statement, "grass is green";

- *events*—things that take place in time that usually involve a change in properties.

So, what does all that mean? Your business glossary should also be organized as your business ontology.

We like to think of ourselves as pragmatic beings and, rather than creating a definition writing method to support this idea using pure philosophical reasoning, we chose a pragmatic method of writing grammatically simple statements that provide clarity and can be learned by anyone with a basic foundation in grammar.

As you have seen in *The Structured Definition*, those simple statements are independently verifiable as being correct or not, while not being overly constrained in form. This differs from the statements that other ontological methods employ, such as *knowledge graphs*[22] that have to enable machine readability. We are human after all!

All organizations operate with many abstract concepts that are complex entities (states of affairs), such as the measures and metrics used for reporting, and the life-cycle stages of products, customers, students, etc. For example, the finance

---

[22] Knowledge graphs are a means of organizing data about concepts and their relationships.

department is concerned with maintaining a general ledger for financial reporting; or a university needs to be clear about when to consider a person as being a student as opposed to an applicant or alumnus.

As the previous case studies have illustrated, the abstract nature of the concepts, combined with the lexical ambiguity of the words used to name them, lead to misunderstandings that introduce risk, which can, in turn, be a significant cost to the organization. (Recall our earlier discussion on *Ambiguity* in this chapter.) Having clear definitions that are structured to create taxonomies (the hierarchies of terms formed by their classifications) and ontologies (the characteristics and relationships of terms) provides a significant step toward closing the semantic gap.

Our method of doing this requires eliciting sufficient knowledge from the organization (see *Knowledge Discovery and Management* covered later in this chapter). This method employs techniques that clarify the naming of business terms (entities) and draw out the relations to other business terms. These techniques include language analysis, discourse between key stakeholders, and crafting simple statements for verification.

Knowledge graphs

Ontologies are the framework from which *knowledge graphs* can be created, so a chapter on knowledge would be incomplete without a section on knowledge graphs.

Knowledge graph as a term was coined in the early 1970s and first made popular in 2012 with the announcement of the Google Knowledge Graph, a huge collection of data harvested in part by a web community from many sources, including Wikipedia, and in part through automated retrieval from across the internet.

A knowledge graph is a visual representation of a *knowledge base,*[23] which is a complex method of integrating structured and unstructured data that is organized as a *semantic network* of related concepts. These relationships are visualized with *nodes* that represent concepts, and *edges* that represent the connections between nodes, together representing knowledge about people, places, objects, events, etc., in the form of *triples.* Triples are a simple three-part representation of natural language clauses—*subject-predicate-object*—created by restricting the verbs to a limited set of relationship types. For example, dog *is-a* mammal, mammal *has-a* vertebrae, etc.

---

[23] A knowledge base is similar to a database but contains expert information that can suggest answers to questions.

When business definitions are written in a structured format, the ontology can be displayed as a business term graph which can be easily derived from the related terms in those definitions. Figure 4 is a visual representation of the three business terms defined earlier in this chapter: employee, part-time employee, and claimant.

intrʌlign

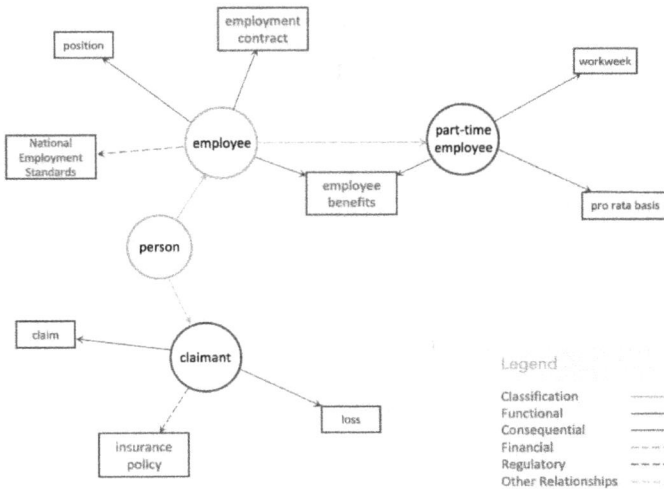

Figure 4 — Business Term Graph

Semantic networks have been used for centuries as a means of visually describing logical reasoning. Recall *Sentence Diagramming*. The field of computer science, which naturally needs to translate complex natural language into a form that is machine-readable, has studied the use of semantic networks and knowledge graphs (the distinction between these terms has become blurred over the last several decades) for computer applications that can infer logic from a network of explicit relations. The most notable applications are internet search engines and voice-recognition question-answering services from Apple, Google, and Amazon.

Also noteworthy are *WordNet*®[24] (because we use it extensively in our own glossary) and *Geonames*. WordNet is an online dictionary that organizes words by synonym sets with senses of meaning, and maps the semantic relationships of *meronymy*,[25] *hyponymy – hypernymy*,[26] and *synonymy*.[27] Geonames is a huge online knowledge graph of geographical places and features.

---

[24] George A. Miller (1995). WordNet: A Lexical Database for English. Communications of the ACM Vol. 38, No. 11: 39-41.
Christiane Fellbaum (1998, ed.) *WordNet: An Electronic Lexical Database.* Cambridge, MA: MIT Press.
WordNet: An Electronic Lexical Database (citation above) is available from http://mitpress.mit.edu/books/wordnet.

[25] A meronym is a term which denotes part of something but is used to refer to the whole, for example, *faces* used to mean *people* in "I see familiar faces."

[26] A hypernym is the class to which the hyponym belongs, such as *cutlery* (hypernym) and *fork* (hyponym).

[27] Synonyms are words or phrases that mean the same or nearly the same as another word or phrase.

Most recently, knowledge graphs are being presented as a faster and more effective way of managing data in organizations. Whether realistic or not, the approach certainly has some proven applications in text analysis. And the ability to apply your organization's taxonomy and ontology to search and catalog data and textual artifacts is an advantage when assessing your risk of information exposure.

Knowledge discovery and management

There's an ongoing debate about whether one-on-one interviews or workshops are a better way to acquire the knowledge you need to effectively capture the business requirements for a project. For general business analysis activities, we recommend choosing the appropriate modality for the situation. However, when establishing definitions of your business terms, there is no better way — and we would posit, no other effective way — than the use of workshops to arrive at consensus from all stakeholders on the appropriate definition of a business term.

When people have to clarify what business terms mean, what their language, jargon, acronyms, and the calculations are, as well as what data feed those calculations in their day-to-day activities, it can be vital to have all stakeholders listening in.

In our experience, core business terms—such as "premium" to an insurance company, or "student" to an educational institution—can carry very diverse meanings and metrics, depending on the context of use within the silos of large organizations. More worryingly, those diverse meanings and metrics can easily go undetected until stakeholders from the various silos are gathered in a room and have to come to a succinct definition of those terms.

Beyond the use of workshops
One concern that is often raised is that of a never-ending workshop cycle. In our experience, once those tricky core terms are defined, the need to run full workshops reduces drastically. But this is only if an effective method of engaging new stakeholders is developed, and your business glossary supports business-friendly online collaboration.

We present further reasoning for using workshops in the section on *Leveraging definition workshops to build community* in Chapter 2, *Sociality*, but for now, in the tables that follow, we list the general pros and cons of the two modalities that are utilized by business analysts (BAs).

Pros	
Workshop	*One-on-One Interview*
When all stakeholders are in the same room, they begin to understand the problems that the ambiguity of their language causes, and the general needs of other stakeholders. The value of this common understanding should not be underestimated.	Allows for all stakeholders to make candid comments without risk of ridicule, shaming, or repercussions from other staff and managers. This can mean greater insight for the BA, and a more honest reflection of the current situation.
While all-in workshops can be a hassle to schedule, they are far less time-consuming for the BA than scheduling many 1:1's, some of which invariably need follow-up meetings for clarification.	Allows for a slow and more detailed description of each stage of the process, which can help the BA get a better handle on the project's scope and end points.
When all stakeholders are in the same room, you begin to develop a community and understanding among them.	Allows the BA to really connect with stakeholders and build trust and buy-in, which can result in better information and more willing participation as the project continues.

Cons	
Workshop	*One-on-One Interview*
Groups can be intimidating for some personalities, which means not all stakeholders will get an equal say. This can mean the BA doesn't get the full picture.	Can be very time-consuming for the BA and draw out the BA's scoping and learning curve timeline for the project.

Cons	
Workshop	*One-on-One Interview*
Some staff will not feel comfortable contradicting management, no matter how mistaken management may be. Again, this can mean the BA doesn't get the full picture.	The community members don't meet together to engage and connect with each other, and they don't get to understand what this project means to other stakeholders. This lack of understanding can undermine a BA's ability to please stakeholders who can only see how the end solution didn't meet their desired outcomes 100%.
Can have little buy-in or engagement from busy or disinterested staff. Staff can feel like the workshop is a big investment of their time for little personal return and may not see the need to know, or be interested in, other participants' views.	The BA may find that multiple interviews are required with certain individuals to clarify matters raised during other conversations. Getting a clear picture of what actually goes on can be harder to ascertain.
Requires excellent facilitation skills and experience, which may not necessarily be within the average BA's skillset.	Language and business term misunderstandings can go unnoticed because the BA is only ever hearing terms in the context of one person's understanding of that term.
	Reviewing and comparing interview notes, collected over many discussions, can be very complex, making it difficult to identify discrepancies.
	Requires excellent memory and fastidious notes.

The following case study shows the benefits of the workshop process, when applied to defining core business terms that are used across the organization and are often misunderstood.

Case study: Defining student in three hours

We previously talked about the effort involved in writing a good definition and the benefits of the workshop process for building connections and consensus. So you might be asking, "Well how long does it take to write a definition?"

We could say, "Well how long is a piece of string?" We won't, because we can tell you, from experience, that a good definition on a key business term that is used across the organization will take on average three hours to define.

That might seem like a long time, but the amount of time wasted in an organization, because everyone assumes that their definition is the only definition, far exceeds that.

We ran a definition workshop at another university here in Australia. The objective of the workshop was to define some of their key metrics, such as "student count", "study load", and "equivalent full-time student load" (known as EFTSL, pronounced "eft-sil"—we think there are more acronyms used in universities than in any other industry.)

Of course, before we could define student metrics, we needed to define *student*. Recall that the Oxford English Dictionary has several definitions:

student | ˈstjuːd(ə)nt |

noun

> a person who is studying at a university or other place of higher
> education: *a **student of** sociology* | *a maths student* | [as modifier]: *student
> loans.*

> • a school pupil: *high-school students.*

> • [as modifier] denoting someone who is studying in order to enter a
>   particular profession: *a group of student nurses.*

> • a person who takes an interest in a particular subject: *a **student of** the free
>   market.*

For a university, the first one works: a person who is studying at a
university or other place of higher education. Easy, let's just use the
dictionary definition. Of course, there was some debate as to
whether they were actually studying!

So why did the university have so many different numbers for
student counts? It turns out each area was counting different sets
of people and calling them all students. One area of the university
included all applicants. Another area excluded applicants and was
only counting students who had actually enrolled in a course or unit
of study. Another area included a portion of the applicants, those
that had accepted an offer, plus all enrolled students. Another
included only enrolled student plus graduates and excluding any
students that deferred their studies.

All these different counts may be correct for their intended
purpose, but when the Vice Chancellor (VC) asks, "how many
students do we have?", which count does the VC want?

The workshop process did highlight that the staff in the different
areas did not have the same view of the student life cycle or an
understanding of what other areas were counting and why. Each
were producing a number to answer a different question.

These numbers were produced for very different purposes:
reaching intake targets, meeting key performance indicators (KPIs),

capacity planning (teaching load), facilities planning, etc. And the financial impact was very different depending on whether you wanted the number as a basis for funding and student contribution versus determining subscription levels for electronic resources. And of course, there was also government reporting to comply with.

Student Recruitment wanted to see that number be as large as possible (meeting their KPIs); Library Services want to see that number be as small as possible as they were charged license fees per student.

The group realized how important it was to know the purpose of the student count and the purpose of the metric became part of the metric's definition. They also realized that they needed a clear picture of what the student life cycle was so that they could qualify all the various stages of a student and know what group of "students" were being counted and for what purpose.

One student term turned into many qualified terms: "prospect", "applicant", "admitted student", "enrolled student", "graduate", etc. Each of these groups of "students" where then further qualified, for example, "commencing students", "continuing students", and "deferred students".

One workshop turned into two, and the university considered those six hours well spent. We not only defined student, but we also identified the various types of students and documented the student life cycle.

Now when someone asks, "How many students do we have?" the response is not just a number. The response is: "What is the question you're trying to answer?"

Summary—Language first

In this chapter, through a number of case studies, we've shown examples of why managing both organizational knowledge and the understanding of business terminology are important factors in reducing risk of infotech project failures and regulatory non-compliance.

We've discussed how structured definitions can help reduce ambiguity, ensure quality content in your business glossary, and be used as a method in definition writing workshops for gaining consensus. In Chapter 2, *Sociality,* we will show how the definition writing workshop process can be used to establish ownership of terms and their definitions.

In the *Seven different numbers for one metric* case study in Chapter 4, *Resources,* we will show how a previously data-driven approach to reporting caused compliance concerns and costly workarounds. Those concerns and workarounds were eliminated by taking a language-driven approach in addressing the data quality issues.

We've also introduced the idea that establishing and managing a business glossary is as much about building and maintaining a community of contributors—governed communities of practice—and users, as it is about capturing knowledge around the terminology used, and how this impacts organizational communication.

An engaged glossary community requires the business communities to develop a set of abilities: *capability* around definition writing and workshopping; *measurability* of definition reuse in producing dashboards and other artifacts; *accountability* and ownership of definitions; and *visibility* of operational issues and business needs that drive the prioritization of knowledge improvement activities. We'll explore these four *abilities* further in the next chapter, *Sociality*.

Management of business terminology is the first step in improving the success of infotech projects and managing other knowledge artifacts, which we'll explore in Chapter 3, *Infotech*, and Chapter 4, *Resources*.

CHAPTER 2

Sociality

"A tribe is a group of people connected to one another, connected to a leader, and connected to an idea. [...] A group needs only two things to be a tribe: a shared interest and a way to communicate. [...]
You can't have a tribe without a leader—and you can't be a leader without a tribe."

Seth Godin[28]

What is sociality?

To build and retain knowledge requires organizational behavior that supports your tribe. Your people deserve access to what they need to succeed, so that you have what you need to succeed. But rather than use the word *tribe*, which is a little passé, we wanted to find a title for this chapter that encompasses the building of a desire to engage within a community that

---

[28] Seth Godin, *Tribes, We Need You to Lead Us*, Piatkus (UK) / Portfolio (USA), 2008.

benefits from improving knowledge. We chose the word *sociality*. The Shorter Oxford English Dictionary defines sociality as:

Noun. 2. The action or fact of forming a society or associating together; the disposition, impulse, or tendency to do this.[29]

In Chapter 1, *Knowledge*, we introduced our *way to communicate*. This chapter is about establishing and reinforcing *shared interest* in what we see as dynamic communities of practice. Our world is facing some pretty amazing technological advances. And our organizations need to adjust and embrace the challenges brought to our world by the advancements and promises of artificial intelligence (AI) and the internet of things (IoT).

Whether or not you watch science fiction, it is relevant to envisioning the future life within any large organization. There's one TV show in particular from which we both enjoy watching the re-runs—Star Trek. If you're not familiar with Star Trek, here's a brief introduction. If you are familiar with Star Trek and its several off-shoots, please feel free to

---

[29] *Shorter Oxford English Dictionary Volume 2,* Fifth edition, Oxford University Press, 2002.

skip this synopsis and our thoughts on the influences from the show's imagined technologies.

Star Trek

Originally started in the 1960s, the premise of Star Trek is that humans have learned to travel faster than light to "explore strange new worlds, seek out new life and new civilizations, to boldly go where no man has gone before." Of course, in the newer spin-off, *Star Trek Next Generation*, the tagline was updated to be the more politically correct "… where no *one* has gone before." The show has inspired generations to develop technologies that were imagined by the writers of that time, for example mobile phones—did you ever own one of the flip-lid variety, like the Motorola Razor? (Mark remembers being allowed to watch the original show, which was screened after his bedtime, by his father during occasions when his mother was at night-school!)

We're unlikely to ever experience being transported ("Beam me up, Scotty!"), although virtual reality-type teleconferencing is pretty amazing. And Lieutenant Data in the Next-Gen series helps us understand some of the ethical dilemmas of artificial intelligence. These ethical questions are real issues today. For example, imagine the scenario where a driverless car must decide whether to drive off a cliff and kill its passengers or plow through several people and save the passengers.

But, getting to the point, the Next-Gen show introduces an alien species called the Borg (no, they're not from Sweden!), who are a cybernetic race of beings that have been assimilated into their "collective" and have a single hive-mind. They announce to those poor beings being assimilated that "resistance is futile!" Obviously inspired by hive organisms, like bees and ants, they are portrayed as being highly efficient and motivated.

Unlike the Borg in *Star Trek*, assimilation into a community of practice is not our intent! But efficiency is a characteristic that we see in any empowered, motivated, and connected community of information curators, led not by a single mind, but by common objectives and a group of business leaders promoting aspects of information governance as a business objective.

The word "governance" tends to instill thoughts of policing and red tape. But if established correctly, governance becomes a vessel for focusing on the issues at hand, encouraging innovation, and navigating the organization around the assimilation imposed by the *data-driven* mantra that was born out of digital disruption and emerging technologies.

In the rest of this chapter, we will focus on shaping the organization's culture to create an effective information management community by:

- establishing and supporting dynamic task-based communities of practice by applying what we covered in Chapter 1, *Knowledge*;

- establishing the right level of information governance over the communities of practice to complement IT's data governance; and

- introducing appropriate organizational change to support the above at a velocity that can be adjusted to suit your organization's appetite to solve business issues caused by lost or missing knowledge and ineffective or badly managed information resources.

Appreciating the importance and value of good information

We don't think anybody would dispute that good information is both valuable and important, and yet it's often not treated with the respect it deserves. Many in the information management profession claim that information is a corporate asset and should be managed as such, in the same way as money and tangible assets. Let's explore this idea, starting with the definition of an asset:

> *"An asset is a resource with economic value that an individual, corporation, or country owns or controls with the expectation that it will provide a future benefit. Assets are reported on a company's balance sheet. They are classified as current, fixed, financial and intangible. They are bought or created to increase a firm's value or benefit the firm's operations."*[30]

---

[30] https://www.investopedia.com/terms/a/asset.asp.

While calling a piece of information an asset sounds plausible, we have yet to find an accountant who has figured out how to express it as a value on the balance sheet. One Chief Data Officer we have spoken with, says that, as well as having potential to be an asset, information can be "a bloody liability!" And we tend to think that this is closer to the truth in most organizations, especially in light of the many examples of data breaches.

Rather than an asset, we think of information as a resource that needs to be managed more like other resources, such as people resources. And while a good manager makes the most of their staff through good management and adherence to policy, the staff should make the most of their information in the same way. In other words, in the same way that an organization has a responsibility of care to its people, its people should have a responsibility of care to its information.

The term we will use throughout this book to refer to information resources is the word *artifact*. The responsibility of care to artifacts is enacted through a process of *curation*.

We will look at artifacts and their curation fully in Chapter 4, *Resources*.

Anecdote: A colleague of ours has this little play example that he gives when presenting on data governance. He rolls an imaginary wheelbarrow into the Chief Financial Officer's office, explains to the audience that the office contains piles of money in various places, and he says, "Hello, I need some money!" to which the CFO replies, "Sure, help yourself." At this point he pretends to shovel the money into the wheelbarrow and leaves the office. He then points out that there are many people who assume that data and information can be freely copied and spread around in piles for others to copy and spread around ad nauseam.

One of the key enablers for managing information resources, and we mean this in the broadest sense of the term to include the people who possess valuable information artifacts, is to have a good classification system—one that is based on common, relevant, and applicable terminology. In our experience, the definition of that terminology is mostly unique within any organization and, once aligned becomes the common language within and between the communities of practice.

Case study—Boeing 737 Max

There had been a lot of discussion in the press about the situation Boeing found itself in following the crashes of its 737 Max aircraft and the grounding of that fleet.

It was a massive human tragedy—346 lives lost! Of course, this was made worse because of its preventable nature. But also, there's no denying that it was a disaster for Boeing's business by any measure.

There are many interesting articles explaining the series of oversights, miscommunications, and assumptions that led to planes with faults being flown by pilots who were not taught what to do if those faults occurred.

Here's what happened.

The 737 Max design is a modified 737NG with more powerful engines. This causes a higher likelihood that the plane could stall more easily in certain situations. To prevent this, the Maneuvring Characteristics Augmentation System (MCAS) was designed to detect and react to a stall. However, it relied on only one of the two angle of attack (AoA) sensors. This introduced risk of erroneous changes to the nose down stabilizer if that one sensor failed. This situation was detected in a test flight but was deemed low risk. There was a procedure for dealing with the situation in flight (should it occur). And it was decided that the procedure did not require a change to the flight manual. Changing the flight manual would have required all existing 737 pilots to undergo conversion training for the Max.

In an industry like aircraft manufacturing, such oversights should not happen. Commercial pressures drove decisions and design shortcuts that were not sufficiently handled by both Boeing and the Federal Aviation Authority (FAA).

In our opinion, Boeing had created a culture of information suppression (where workers, who raised concerns about quality and safety, allegedly experienced disciplinary action). This culture created an environment where serious issues could be missed.

A culture that embraces information governance would have provided all staff a level of visibility of the steps undertaken and decisions made by staff at every stage of the plane's design and development process. This visibility would (if the right culture existed in Boeing) have allowed staff to raise their concerns, so that quality and safety issues were seen, understood, and addressed in the development phase—not in the once-the-plane-has-crashed phase.

If the issue-raising process itself had equally adequate governance, those with the knowledge and power to solve those issues would have routinely been made aware of the issues. And they would have been given accountability to ensure the issues were satisfactorily resolved, greatly decreasing the likelihood of the plane being flawed.

When someone suggested that the risk rating of the MCAS should be raised, this would have prompted additional safety reviews. Also, the decision to not update the manual on how to recognize and react to an MCAS failure would have been challenged.

Ultimately, it was a poor company culture, driven by competitive pressure to deliver the plane to market as quickly as possible which led to several pieces of vital information falling through the cracks.

A culture that values information and visibility would have ensured this could not happen, or at least, ensured it was far, far less likely that these tragedies would occur. In this case, it could have meant hundreds of people still being alive today.

For most businesses, a poor culture or process blind spots won't result in the loss of human life, but the risk they do face can still represent significant financial loss, legal implications, and reputational damage.

And that should be a concern for all business leaders.

Organizational change

Your organization may have recently gone through, or may be currently performing, a transformation program. The cultural change needed to establish sociality can happen gradually; it doesn't need a huge corporate program, but it must be promoted from the top. And not necessarily the top of the organization—we have seen situations where the leader of a department has driven change at their level, thereby creating peer envy which caused change more broadly.

There are four aspects needed to build and maintain the required cultural change:

- Leadership—any successful community of practice must have *accountability* in the form of a leader. That leader must lead staff to become aware of the need to build, share and maintain knowledge and fully support the community in building *capability* with appropriate tools and skills, especially soft skills.

- Education—changing culture in an organization is rarely easy. But with appropriate examples, people can begin to appreciate the way they treat data and information can adversely affect their colleagues across the organization. Of course, there will be political barriers—knowledge is power, in this case being in control of information artifacts. These barriers can be overcome with clear mandates from, and formal agreement between, the organizational leaders.

- Language –As mentioned already, having a way to communicate is an essential feature of a community, and a shared language is the core of any community, in this case, the community of highly effective information curators.

- Information issues —*visibility* of business issues allows their prioritization. To know what issues exist, the organization must develop a no-blame culture and awareness of individual responsibility to raise any perceived issue. The resolution of each issue then becomes the focal point of the cultural change, through the understanding and agreement of what it is (its definition) and the activities of working together toward its resolution. And having *measurability* of issue cost and resolution benefit provides validation.

Business-driven information management culture

Establishing a culture that values information management (IM) as part of the business community is key to:

- improving the quality of information available, especially key metrics;

- capturing and disseminating business knowledge of key processes and resources within business areas; and

- capturing the true meaning of business terminology and disseminating it within and between business areas.

Doing this ultimately leads to improved performance and better-informed investment in infotech projects. It also reduces the risk of losing valuable knowledge from people that could otherwise walk out the door and take that knowledge with them. We've already mentioned establishing *visibility*, which directly affects the reliability of the information used for operational and regulatory reporting. If you want quality information and reliable metrics on your business, the whole organization must be given the ability to raise issues without fear of retribution and, perhaps, even rewarded for doing so.

When Mark worked in the petrochemical industry, the company had a "Coin Your Ideas" reward program, where employees could make process suggestions to improve performance and safety. Each idea was evaluated for its cost and benefit, and if implemented, a percentage of the benefit would end up in the employee's wages.

Horst Schulze is seen as a guru in developing a culture of service in the hotel industry. He is co-founder of the Ritz-

Carlton Hotel Company and oversaw its rise to prominence in the luxury hotel market. Horst Schulze had taken a more proactive approach. Rather than a rewards program for ideas, he enacted an empowerment program.

In a podcast hosted by Donald Miller, Schulze talks about the methodology they employed to improve the experience of their customers' stay at their hotels.[31] This included empowering all staff to solve customer problems, even those at the bottom of the hierarchy, such as cleaners and service staff. They were given the responsibility and capability to ensure the resolution of those problems. Staff had the resources they needed to solve certain problems without even requesting approval, including a budget of two thousand dollars to solve customer problems on the spot.

To create this kind of business culture, it must be modeled by executive staff and rolled down through management. Solve and resolve, don't tolerate and mitigate.

Organizational culture shapes the way employees handle problems, make decisions, and interact with one another.

[31] Miller, Donald (host). Podcast #133 "*Horst Schulze – How to lead with vision so your brand stands out.*" Building a Storybrand with Donald Miller | Clarify your message so customers will listen. 28 Jan 2019. Available on iTunes. Accessed 30 Jan 2019.

Employee turnover is almost always a symptom of a bad workplace culture and results in lost organizational knowledge. Ignoring the lost knowledge, just the cost of hiring a new employee can be very costly, as we can see in the following case study.

Case study—Amazon's Staff Attrition

Internal documents, including a paper published in January 2022, leaked to Engadget,[32] indicate that worldwide employee attrition has an estimated cost to Amazon and its shareholders of $8 billion annually, more than 25% of their stated profit of $33.36 billion for the 2021 fiscal year.

Between 69.5% and 81.3% of the staff attrition, measured across all levels of employment, is attributed to workers who leave the company of their own volition. They also note that "'only one out of three new hires in 2021'" stay with the company for 90 or more days.'

Amazon, no doubt, has very well-documented processes, so the loss of staff probably doesn't adversely impact organizational memory. But it does indicate cultural and workplace problems and would certainly lead to other costs.

---

[32] A. Menegus, *Exclusive: Amazon's attrition costs $8 billion annually according to leaked documents. And it gets worse.* Engadget, October 17, 2022 https://www.engadget.com/amazon-attrition-leadership-ctsmd-201800110.html.

3Rs—Roles, responsibilities, and rewards

Good information management requires a culture that values information and can protect and share information responsibly for the benefit of the whole organization. A good information culture will also acknowledge that data and information are not the same. It is possible to have good data management (that is, the management of the content of databases and operational files) and still have poor information management. For example, creating a report from sensitive data and then allowing it to be exposed to people, or for purposes, beyond the stated objective, either deliberately, accidentally, or naively.

A successful information management culture is one in which everyone understands the principle of ownership. That is, everyone knows their own accountability or responsibility for a specific information artifact and can easily identify those who are accountable or responsible for any other specific information artifact, such as a data set. It is also one that has information management principles that are clearly mandated from the top and supported by sufficient and appropriate education. It is not enough to have a governance framework that dictates roles and responsibilities without providing the appropriate education and capabilities for employees to fulfill those roles and responsibilities.

> *Information governance roles and responsibilities do not constitute new positions but rather become aspects of existing positions.*

It's important to establish a reward system up front; perhaps tied to the issues being raised, or based on the value of the resolution of the issue, or even based on the most significant issue raised each period. Just be mindful that incentivizing the wrong way can lead to bad behaviors.

One good incentive method we've seen is tying rewards to charitable donations. That way, the staff will feel good about not only solving an internal issue, but, at the same time, contributing to a good cause.

Best practice information management also requires good control over information management tools and capabilities, whereby data and information storage are not siloed, but also not centrally owned or managed by IT in the same way as operational systems and data. A strategy of a centralized core environment, with appropriate-level controls and capabilities to support and manage federated activities, is in line with best practice.

Investing in education, not just technology

Organizations continue to invest heavily in technologies like cloud computing, the *internet of things* (IoT), and artificial intelligence (AI). According to Zion Market Research, the global AI industry should grow to $422.37 billion by 2028, as compared to $59.67 billion in 2021.[33]

Forecast like this are one of the reasons why organizations are biased toward investing in developing technical skills, causing an imbalance with what is known as power skills— also known as interpersonal skills or soft skills, such as communication, problem-solving, and collaborative leadership.

Investing more in establishing business information management capability, and applying the KSIR strategy, will reduce the risk of ineffective technology spend because the business community will be better equipped with power skills to manage their information artifacts and make informed decisions over infotech investment.

Despite the need for these critical power skills, research shows that organizations are spending only one-quarter (25%) of their annual budget for training and development in these skills versus more than half (51%) spent on

---

[33] Forbes, How to Invest in Artificial Intelligence, Jan 2023, https://www.forbes.com/sites/qai/2022/10/05/how-to-invest-in-artificial-intelligence/.

technical skills training, such as in methods like Agile and the use of technical tools.[34]

Another survey conducted by PMI (2020) asked senior executives what they expected to make the most investment in over the next 3-5 years. The survey revealed that 49% expected considerable investment in technology advancements, 44% in digitalization, while only 24% expected to invest in human capital/talent development (training).[35]

Leveraging definition workshops to build community

In Chapter 1, *Knowledge*, in the section *Knowledge Discovery and Management*, we said when establishing definitions of your business terms there is no better way than to use workshops—and we would posit, no other effective way—than the use of workshops to arrive at consensus from all

---

[34] Project Management Institute (2023), *Pulse of the Profession® - Power Skills, Redefining Project Success*, 14th Edition, https://www.pmi.org/-/media/pmi/documents/public/pdf/learning/thought-leadership/pmi-pulse-of-the-profession-2023-report.pdf.

[35] Project Management Institute (2020), *Pulse of the Profession® - Ahead of the Curve: Forging a Future-Focused Culture*, Appendix - Section 2.

stakeholders on the appropriate definition of a business term.

But more than this, there are deeper benefits your organization will experience from doing this definitional work via workshops, which involves the building of community across silos (business functional areas). In turn, this community building can have knock-on benefits, as corporate knowledge of the work of other silos deepens, and cross-silo relationships are fostered. This leads to greater opportunities for collaborative work, the leveraging of resources and expertise, and the building of greater capacity for the organization as a whole.

Workshop attendees are essentially a dynamic community of practice, established for the subjects being discussed. This membership must be recorded so that communication about the related subjects can occur between the respective communities.

Benefits of business term definition workshops

When all stakeholders are brought together, they begin to understand the full scope of activity across the organization, the complexities in the use of language in each area, and the reasons a unified language is important. This can build a shared sense of problem-solving and purpose as participants realize they're contributing to something necessary and valuable.

While large workshops can be a hassle to schedule, having all stakeholders together means that discussion and debate, over suggested definitions, happen in real time, and problems are raised and resolved far more quickly than they could be in one-on-one interviews. Workshops therefore end up being far less time-consuming for your governance and business term definition team than any other method of consensus.

When all stakeholders are participating, you begin to develop community and understanding among them about their information needs and the difficulties faced by each business functional area. Those difficulties and needs are revealed as the group agree on a definition that works for all, and the ground becomes fertile for cross-functional area collaboration. Relationships are built, faces are put to names, and personalities to faces, which helps put participants at ease with each other and engage further in conversation outside of the meeting. This can organically grow the scope of collaboration, resource sharing, and even cost saving on projects or resource spending.

From the perspective of your business term definition writing team, workshops offer the fastest and most time-efficient route to clarity around the key business terms that are often the most difficult because they have the most diverse use across the organization.

These key terms are usually the most commonly used; they carry the most assumed knowledge, which is often the cause of ambiguity. Once your stakeholders begin to see a definition forming, question it, come back to it, realize the initial definition doesn't fulfill requirements, and circle back to it, workshop facilitators and attendees will begin to see the true value of having all the stakeholders involved as these subsequent considerations are raised.

To have over 20 stakeholders being approached in one-on-one meetings, then re-consulted with later amendments, only to make their own further amendments, and so on and so on, is simply impractical and untenable for the time allowance most staff have for this work.

A number of three-hour or four-hour workshops, with all participants, over a matter of weeks, seems like a huge commitment. But in reality, this can result in far less person-hours overall, lower cost for the organization, and be more effective for your definition writing team.

Effective workshop facilitation

The main drawback of workshops is that domineering personalities can (inadvertently and sometimes without facilitators noticing) intimidate other attendees. This can prevent the raising of comments, suggestions, or objections. This, of course, undermines the effectiveness of the final definition. It also defeats the purpose of a workshop as a tool for encouraging the breakdown of silos and fostering collaborative communities.

Therefore, facilitators must be skilled in workshop preparation and facilitation, so that they're comfortable and able to ask all participants for input, reign in over-zealous or intimidating participants, and foster a safe space for discussion and exploration of ideas. This may mean establishing workshop ground rules, using playful ways to bring order back to an unruly discussion, and challenging the absolute statements made by stronger or more vocal participants — on behalf of those who may be quieter or less willing to challenge the dominant opinions.

It also behooves the facilitator to work at developing relationships with each participant individually, so that those with reservations know and feel comfortable approaching the facilitator privately. This would encourage them to air any concerns they may have about the definition, which they would prefer not to raise in the group setting.

This scenario is one of the primary reasons many people prefer using one-on-one interviews over workshops. However, it is our view that workshops are still preferable, and if facilitators can develop the trust of quieter participants, concerns can be taken back to the group at the next workshop by the facilitator for further discussion. This can actually result in the quieter individual growing in their confidence at raising future issues when they see others in the group agreeing with the problems they raised in private.

Poorly facilitated workshops can end up being detrimental to the overall outcomes of the definition writing process, so we encourage businesses to train and upskill their definition writing staff.

Overcoming resistance

When staff are invited to one or more three-hour or four-hour workshops, there can be a natural resistance to participation.

Those organizing the workshops and sending the invitations must be very clear about why the business term definition writing process is important to the invitee. If stakeholders do not see or understand the relevance of the workshop to their role, business functional area, or responsibility, they are likely to be resistant.

Also, invitees are far more likely to be happy to attend when the culture of the organization, and in particular the promotion and encouragement to do the work of information management, is seen and heard regularly from the business leaders. Managers are also more likely to encourage their staff to participate rather than block engagement for what they may see as competing for resources.

Ensuring the meetings are relaxed and enjoyable, with appropriately sized meeting rooms, the provision of refreshments, and allowance for sufficient breaks is essential for in-person workshops. But we have also run many successful *virtual* workshops, provided certain meeting protocols are employed, such as cameras on and being present.

We have found that there is little resistance to workshops, providing the attendees' initial experiences are all positive. This can be achieved through well-crafted invitations, having their questions and concerns answered, and participation in a successful, well-run first workshop.

This last case study for the chapter illustrates how cultural beliefs over resource ownership were challenged, how the workshop process brought the business community together, and how information governance led to successful outcomes for an organization and its clients.

Case study—Health screening

The client, a government health organization, provides free breast screening services for women aged 40 years and over. The purpose is to detect breast cancer in its early stages when treatment could be most effective.

In 2013, there were 43 breast screening sites (including hospital campuses) and 13 mobile vans, which visited around 160 locations, across 8 Local Health Districts (LHDs). Each of the 8 LHDs that were providing screening and assessment services maintained their own independent processes and systems to capture information about a client and the screening service provided. Needless to say, each collected the data inconsistently, which made it difficult to assess client outcomes, and nearly impossible when the client attended different screening sites, because their information was not shared across LHDs.

The central office recognized that a single system would solve many of the data issues, as well as the issues of transferring information between LHDs and to the central office. The central office was responsible for the funding and oversight of the program and also provided data to researchers. So, a program of work was established to standardize the administrative processes and improve the quality of the information collected. The goal: one system to rule them all.

The business case ticked all the right boxes. It promised to: improve data collection; reduce duplication; improve efficiencies; reduce admin costs; improve marketing and recruitment activities; and, most importantly, improve the quality of the assessment services. What happened in the initial phase was the implementation of an Electronic Health Record (EHR) system. But this system was customized for each of the unique processes in each of the eight LHDs. Yes, they had one platform, one system, but eight unique instances of that system. Unification and standardization didn't happen.

Unfortunately, part of the business case for the new system was to reduce the staff in each of the LHDs. One of the biggest mistakes was to ignore the value of the data managers in each of the LHDs. We loved the fact that they had data managers and that their job title was data manager. You didn't find that in many corporate organizations at that time. The central office believed, having one system, they could administer it with a much smaller team in the central office and reduce admin costs. Sounds great, doesn't it? What they didn't realize was that each data manager understood the nuances of the processes and the clients in their own LHD. They performed more than just "administrative" tasks; they ensured that the data collected was accurate. This required follow-up with the client, and the ability to build relationships with medical staff doing the assessments, the admin staff inputting data, and the clients. Connection and coordination within a given LHD was strong. The connection that was weak was between the LHDs and the central office.

The central office realized that the only way to achieve the benefits promised in the business case was to establish a governance framework under which the eight LHDs and the central office could operate. As a government agency, frameworks, policies, and procedures are the norm. As a health agency, information privacy and security are paramount. The challenge was getting collaboration and agreement across the LHDs, as well as between the LHDs and central office. This required aligning the procedures and determining the roles and responsibilities that fell within each of the LHDs and those of the central office. This required getting everyone together and talking, without the threat of being made redundant. Collaboration and alignment didn't happen overnight. It took ten months and several facilitated workshops to understand the processes, how they differed, why they differed, and the challenges that would be faced by the staff in getting those processes and the language aligned.

One thing we found that helped with the dynamics of the group was to have an independent facilitator—one that was not part of any LHD or the central office and, especially, one that was not from the vendor providing the system. (The original requirements sessions with the eight LHDs were led by the vendor and resulted in eight unique instances of the system, with little alignment.)

Another thing that helped was that they all passionately agreed on one thing—the value of the screening service they provided. Reinforcing that common goal allowed the group to remain active and engaged. They were defining how they would work together and who had responsibility for what. This was governance in action, not dictated by a "framework" document. The end result was a collaborative working group of data managers across the LHDs, as well as a governance framework containing agreed standards, roles and responsibilities, and governance processes that could be measured.

An added benefit to the central office was that it laid a foundation which enabled the planned consolidation of other cancer screening and assessment operations. It also enabled the restructure of the information management and reporting processes in both the LHDs and the central office. The LHDs had also benefitted from a review of the metrics that had been used to allocate funding and assess the program's success. The LHDs had complained about the metrics for some time but had been unable to provide supporting evidence that the metrics were flawed. The new reporting environment gave everyone a more accurate and transparent view of the program's success.

Summary

This chapter has focused on culture and how it affects organizations, both positively and negatively. We've presented practical ways for using knowledge-sharing definition workshops to provide an environment that nurtures the establishment of communities of practice. We've also noted that these communities need educational support to build capability. And we've discussed ways of establishing a cultural change to support information management as a business function. We continue on this topic in the next chapter, which examines why this cultural change must occur.

And in Chapter 4, *Resources*, we will provide a case study, Seven different numbers for one metric, about a Chief Financial Officer (CFO) of a telecommunications company who was getting conflicting numbers for a key metric. In that case study, we will illustrate how information quality improvement must have a foundation that includes cultural change.

CHAPTER 3

Infotech

"A fool with a tool is still a fool."

Grady Booch

The information technology (infotech) strategic landscape has changed dramatically since COVID-19 caused lockdowns. It resulted in mandated virtual working conditions which drove improvements to personal video conferencing and collaboration through technology. It also stressed an urgent, increased need for online education and commerce. However, some infotech strategies remain unchanged: system consolidation around billing and enterprise resource planning (ERP) systems; and data management and analytics.

As pointed out in Chapter 1, *Knowledge*, 34% of project failures are due to having focused on the solution—without sufficient alignment with business requirements. In this chapter, we look at how the focus on system consolidation solutions often ignore the impacts on business operations, ultimately resulting in overruns on budget, questionable return on investment, and frustrated employees.

We also look at the current approaches in the areas of data management and analytics, and their potential to impact organizations negatively, especially when system consolidation is attempted. We will explore enterprise data architecture—data models and platforms—and how these are often driven by opinion, or a data strategy, that's not aligned with the broader organizational strategy and capabilities.

We will also consider the history and evolution of infotech and propose an alternative approach to information management that addresses many of today's challenges.

In Chapter 1, *Knowledge*, we gave examples of how business language (terms and definitions) affects infotech projects. The case studies in this chapter will illustrate how the lack of business-led information management can result in ineffective infotech investment. We will also show how the right approach saves money and, in one case study, potentially saved the company.

The need for systems thinking

Mark's undergraduate studies were heavily systems-oriented and his approach to leadership and business activities includes systems thinking. An organization is a system, not a collection of independent components, so any change to one component will affect the system as a whole—and not necessarily in a positive way. For example, a new ERP system will require a huge effort in data quality, data migration, and replacement of reporting systems. This effort is rarely, if ever, budgeted for or planned appropriately.

Our observation is that organizational leaders, and especially those driving enterprise data strategy, are often unaware of the impact of their decisions to other areas of the organization. Yet, despite lack of progress, they continue to apply the same data strategy, because it is promoted by the infotech industry as *best practice*.

The infotech industry—particularly in the data space—is incredibly versatile in creating new names for old concepts, spruiking and spinning success stories, and luring in the technologists with those shiny new toys.

Don't misunderstand—some interesting and exciting new technologies can provide strategic advantage, but only for organizations that are mature enough to execute them effectively.

However, we've watched the cycle of misaligned strategies repeat over the years, just like in the Groundhog Day movie, only nothing really changes. As the saying goes, often attributed to Albert Einstein, "the definition of insanity is doing the same thing over and over and expecting a different result."

This has been summarized nicely in the following statement made by Russel L. Ackoff during a lecture:

"Wisdom makes the transition between efficiency and effectiveness because it evaluates the end which we're pursuing efficiently.
The distinction is contained in a wonderful statement by Peter Drucker, who once said, 'There's a big difference between doing things right, and doing the right thing.' You see, we are very largely devoted to doing the wrong thing, right. That's very unfortunate because the righter you do the wrong thing, the wronger you become! When we do the right thing wrong, we make a mistake, which when detected, allows us to improve."[36]

Infotech evolution

Before digital computing emerged in business, there were no IT departments or information management functions (also called data management). Information was handled by business process—business people wrote down information on forms and in documents. These were filed in filing cabinets by filing clerks and, when there was a need to analyze data, the filing department would retrieve the relevant files and either perform, or issue them for, the

---

[36] Russell L. Ackoff, *Systems Thinking, Learning, and Problem Solving,* https://www.youtube.com/watch?v=O9TE9HWFo6U.

analysis. Those filing clerks knew what information existed and how it was stored.

When digital computing emerged, information technology replaced the filing cabinets and filing techniques. Over time, due to the technical nature of running digital equipment, it was assumed by the business people that the responsibility for information management—how the information is captured, stored, retrieved, presented for analysis, and archived—would also fall to the IT department (then called Information Technology *Services* or ITS). No longer were there filing clerks, although a similar role—the librarian—continued to exist, handling both printed and digital records and publications.

As IT resources—hardware and software, not the information flows or people talent—are becoming more like appliances (as predicted in the highly critiqued 2004 book, *Does IT Matter?* by Nicholas G Carr), they are becoming more ubiquitous, easier to use, and readily accessible via *software as a service* (SaaS). We have also noticed that business people tend to be more tech-savvy from their business degrees and experience, whereas IT professionals tend not to be more business savvy from their technology degrees and experience.

With IT best practices continually evolving openly through online communities, magazines, and tutorials, technical knowledge becomes easily accessible to both IT and business professionals. Considering the increasing level of IT outsourcing, IT professionals are being driven to continually update their technical skills and work portfolios, but there is no corresponding driver to increase their business knowledge. Competitive advantage is no longer about access to infotech but about business acumen.

Business-led information management

In Chapter 2, *Sociality*, we introduced the idea of establishing a business-driven information management culture. Having looked at the infotech evolution, we've seen how the business community relinquished responsibility for information management to IT. It's time for the business community to take back that responsibility.

We're not advocating the abolishment of information management as an IT function. It is quite appropriate for IT to manage certain aspects of data management, such as security and design methods and functions, particularly when dealing with structured data—data stored in databases. One of the arguments we hear too often from the IT community is that the business people aren't disciplined enough, or don't have enough understanding or capability, to perform information management. On the other hand, we often hear from the business community that IT does not have sufficient business acumen.

Smart companies realize that product and process innovation are key to advantage. With that said, who would you rather trust with your organizational data, information, and knowledge? This is the crux of the *data-driven-business* mantra. We should instead be promoting *business-driven data* based on effective and sustainable business-led information management processes.

This is where the KSIR strategy shines, rebuilding business maturity for effective evaluation of, and informed infotech investment in, anything to do with data.

We would, therefore, argue that, rather than continuing to put all information-related activities under the Chief Information Officer (CIO), business people are in a better position to re-establish responsibility for:

- specifying their information needs using clearly defined business terminology;

- the management of conceptual-level enterprise data models; and

- organizing and managing the information resources that they use, such as: reports, dashboards, spreadsheets, policies, procedures, documents, etc. —what we call *information artifacts*.

Information artifacts are often referred to as *unstructured data* or *semi-structured data* by IT professionals.

Information artifacts, along with a business-managed glossary of business terms, represent the explicit knowledge of the organization's business operations. Without proper management of this knowledge by people who understand the core business processes (but not necessarily the technology), including all the undocumented workarounds, the organization will remain at risk of:

- lost organizational knowledge due to staff attrition,
- broken business processes,
- regulatory non-compliance, and
- ineffective infotech investment.

As a risk mitigation strategy, the building of these information management capabilities and accountabilities sits well under the Chief Risk Officer (CRO), Chief Financial Officer (CFO), or Chief Operations Officer (COO).

Chapter 1, *Knowledge*, presented some research on how much money is spent on infotech projects and their failures. The following case study illustrates how money was inappropriately invested into infotech, where the Chief Data and Analytics Officer (CDAO) essentially doubled down on his strategy to establish a new data analytics platform.

Case study—Data and analytics misaligned with business needs

The Australian branch of a large multinational insurance company invested in building a data analytics environment. One of the key business benefits promoted by the Chief Data and Analytics Officer was a single customer view.

This appealed broadly to the business community; in particular to the commercial insurance team, being the largest revenue segment with the most to gain from understanding how their commercial clients may be related in terms of parent-subsidiaries and conglomerate corporations. Understanding these structures would provide opportunities for analysis and marketing.

However, the data-analytics platform program prioritized the personal insurance line of business but did include a data quality program to improve the capture of Australian Company Number (ACN) and Australian Business Number (ABN) data for the commercial line of business. The analytics group incorrectly believed that ABN and ACN would be a step improvement for the single customer view for commercial business. This assumption had two flaws:

-   ABNs and ACNs are unique to each legal entity in the structure and those entities cannot be related reliably even if the company names are similar.

-   Most commercial insurance is sold through brokers. The contracts with the brokers do not include the provision of client data beyond what is needed for the insurance policy. This allows the brokers to protect their client data, thereby preventing the insurance company from directly marketing to those clients. One result is that the ABN or ACN provided is that of the broker!

Despite the flaws outlined above, data quality metrics were reported regularly and provided little more than format compliance.

The project did not deliver the promised return on investment.

Data models

We're going to assume you don't know much about data models and how they sit in the organizational landscape. But even if you do, we want to share some observations that we have made. In this section, we provide an overview of the types of data models and the ones that you should be aware of as a business leader or manager.

Business users can use data models. We produced a data warehouse logical data model for a medium-sized telecommunications company by working with a cross-section of their business community. The marketing department had it on the wall and used it when talking about market analysis. The company was about to embark on an expensive billing system consolidation, driven by the parent company's choice of technology. Using the data model, it was explained to IT that the new system could not be configured for mobile products. The IT project was canceled and we're sure that saved more than a lot of money!

Business Information models

We've already discussed business language as being core to organizational knowledge in Chapter 1, *Knowledge*, and how clear, structured definitions of key business concepts are crucial to avoiding ambiguity in communication and, especially, in infotech system architecture and design. In reference to the infotech needs, business concepts are typically presented as a business information model.[37]

Data quality and enterprise architecture frameworks will mandate having an enterprise data model (EDM). This is classically an IT artifact and is usually presented as an entity-relationship diagram. However, we rarely see an organization that has successfully produced an EDM that is accessible, validated, and maintained with input from the business community.

One argument that we have heard against building an EDM is that it requires too much effort over a long period and provides little demonstrable value. Also, as data modeling is considered a *design* methodology and skill,[38] it is argued that data modeling is generally incompatible with Agile working methods. In fact, data modelers were too often dropped from the IT development process and even the payroll; a decision that we are currently seeing reversed due to the costly impact of not employing experienced data modelers in infotech projects.

---

[37] The term conceptual data model is often used but it is ambiguous: "There are many different published definitions for the term conceptual data model..." — Graham Witt, *Data Modeling for Quality*, Technics Publications, 2021.

[38] Graeme Simsion, *Data Modeling Theory and Practice*, Technics Publications LLC, 2007.

> *Often, the perceived alternative to creating an EDM is to purchase an industry reference model, which we don't recommend in any solution—these models should only be considered as a general reference for the data modeler. We discuss industry data models later in this chapter.*

Noting that data modeling is a design process, not a descriptive process, an alternative way of depicting a business information model is by starting with a definitional approach in natural language, which is exactly what we discussed in Chapter 1, *Knowledge*. This alternative overcomes the argument of not being compatible with Agile development methods. By focusing on the business terminology that forms the basis of the project, their structured definitions can be agreed quickly and used as a basis for rapid design of the project's data models. The definitions can also be used as the basis of an evolving EDM. These statements are valid, providing that the ontological relationships between business terms (concepts) used in the definitions are exposed. This would be achieved with a well-structured glossary, using Wikipedia-like navigation.

We produced such a business glossary for a life-insurance company. They acknowledged that their enterprise data modeler was able to create the data models for their enterprise data warehouse more rapidly with the aid of the glossary. The data modeler was able to analyze the concept-relationships in the structured definitions, rather than seeking validation from the business subject-matter experts after each design iteration of the model.

Data catalog and data governance tools are typically focused on data in systems. While they often come with a business glossary, it will be implemented primarily to help search for data. These glossaries do not easily provide the ontological relationships between business terms. They misconstrue the complex relationships that describe how the data relates to the business terms, do not align with the needs of language governance (which are different from those of data governance), and are limited in their ability to support business management of the glossary. Remember that business language maintains some level of currency, whereas data structures are based on some degree of historical application design.

Logical and physical data models and architectures

The business information model, as described above, is generally the precursor to a *logical data model* (LDM), which provides a more detailed (fully *attributed*) and technology-agnostic design. The actual data storage (schema) for a system is a physical data model (PDM). This design reflects known constraints of the chosen technology and consideration for the expected data access needs.

An enterprise logical data model (eLDM) represents the data needs of the enterprise. It is usually the design basis for the enterprise data warehouse, which is the central location for analyzing data.

> *There are many ways to manage data in one place to support analysis. The names used include: "data warehouse," "data lake," "data lakehouse," "data fabric," and, more generally, just "big data." Each of these have different methods of structuring the data but try to achieve the same purpose: to get data that is stored in different ways, with different names, from multiple operational systems, and bring that data together in one place. This data then needs some level of consistent representation, in order to provide a means to analyze and report on the organization's current and historical operations and performance. Despite these different approaches, we will focus on the original concept and name: "data warehouse."*

The physical data model is the subject of fierce debates in data warehouse design, and there are three main competing design concepts: Dan Linstedt's *data vault*; Bill Inmon's *normalized modeling*; and Ralph Kimball's *dimensional modeling*.

These design concepts also mandate different data processing methods. The processing methods are generally referred to as a sequence involving extracting data, transforming data, and loading data. The order in which these occur are either extract-transform-load (ETL) or extract-load-transform (ELT). The design concepts and the processing methods together form part of the data warehouse *architecture*:

- Data vault is very much about ingesting data more rapidly, using repeatable templates, while maintaining auditability about where and when the data was sourced. It is designed for quickly adding new data without having to change existing structures in the physical data model. It is quite complex and requires well-skilled data professionals to ensure correct design and to analyze source data for correct loading. Subsequently, the data must be extracted and transformed to load more usable structures, for example, the *business vault*. The business vault provides a less complex structure as a next step to provide support for reporting and analysis.

- Kimball architecture, which performs well on most database technologies, provides a relatively quick implementation for answering standard questions and feeding business intelligence reports. The Kimball architecture uses fact and dimension tables in its physical model. Fact tables contain business events—orders, shipments, payments, etc.—and the associated measures—dollar amounts, quantities, etc. Dimension tables provide the who, what, when, where, why, and how, used to aggregate data in the fact table. These structures are arguably easier to understand than normalized entity-relationship (ER) designs although "... a dimensional model is just a restricted form of an ER model."[39]

- Inmon architecture uses a normalized design, which increases the number of tables, as it requires splitting out functionally dependent data into separate tables. The objective of normalization is to minimize data redundancy (Codd, 1970). This design requires *integrated* data — data with the same concept from different sources is standardized through complex transformation. Data integration takes time and money to develop and maintain. However, the integrated database can be used to explore scenarios that were unknown at design time. This was the preferred architecture for Teradata's massive parallel processing (MPP) database since its inception in 1979, being one of the few technologies that can offer high performance against normalized data and scale to support very large data warehouses.

Debating and choosing an architecture are often based on IT architectural dogma. Yet each of the architectures offers a

---

[39] Moody, Daniel L. and Kortink, Mark A.R, From ER Models to Star Schemas: Mapping From Operational Databases to Data Warehouse Designs (2003). ACIS 2003 Proceedings. 65. https://aisel.aisnet.org/acis2003/65.

solution to one of three different strategic needs: speed of ingestion, speed of delivery, or quality and consistency of data, respectively.

The data strategy, and its data architecture, must align with the organization's strategic goals and the business needs to achieve those goals. Those business needs will often require different data architectures for different reasons. As an example, consider a financial organization's need for fraud detection versus its marketing objectives:

- Fraud detection will likely be based on known and emerging scenarios requiring rapid ingestion and analysis, so the data architecture must be designed accordingly.

- The marketing department's needs may require more ad hoc analysis, and they could likely support longer development cycles. Therefore, a more normalized strategic data architecture may be more suitable. But this should be considered in conjunction with a design to ingest data from multiple systems in order to build history as a first stage process. The development of the strategic architecture could then be prioritized.

Industry data models

A common vendor data-driven solution, that claims to avoid producing an enterprise data model, is the industry data model. We have experience with these models in the insurance, banking, telecommunications, and transportation industries. Industry models are too generic and ambiguous, and often conflict with the terminology used by the organization. This is because they are built based on the vendor's knowledge of the industry, as operated in specific countries, and they compromise on the different terminologies in use *across* organizations, even though they are in the *same* industry—no two organizations in the same industry are the same!

Implementing an industry model as the design basis for a data warehouse will lead to confusion, for both the data engineers and the users, resulting in questionable return on investment.

In our telecommunications case study, *Seven different numbers for one metric*, detailed in Chapter 4, *Resources*, the CFO was getting conflicting data for a metric needed for regulatory reporting. That organization had implemented a data warehouse using an infotech vendor's industry data model, as approved by the enterprise architecture group. Over four years, they had subsequently spent millions of dollars in several unsuccessful attempts to address the issue.

The industry model was identified as one of three reasons behind the issue.

Data and information quality

Data quality or, as we prefer to call it, information quality, is a hot topic already addressed by many books. So, we won't be exploring this area too deeply. However, we will provide our observations, along with a couple of case studies, illustrating good information quality practices and practices to be aware of.

There are plenty of debates over the terms "data" and "information", especially when used as an adjective, such as in data quality and information quality, and they are often used interchangeably. Our personal preference is to use the term data when referring to structured, machine-readable forms, and the term information as a broader term. The broader term extends into the world of what is called unstructured data or semi-structured data by the information technologists and includes documents and reports, etc., that we refer to as information artifacts.

Information quality has always been considered a part of data management practice, but this has been questioned, most notably by the late Larry P English, who, as a pioneer, is considered to be the *father of information quality*. To quote Larry:

> *"Information Management (or Information Resource Management) is a distinct discipline associated with business management. Information Quality Management is a general Management Tool that is used to design quality into processes to error-proof them and ensure that the processes meet Customer Requirements, whether Manufacturing, Service Delivery or Information Capture, Maintenance and Delivery. I fear that the Information Management (most call it Data Management) function has been usurped as an IT Technical specialty."[40]*

We were both lucky enough to work alongside Larry as we implemented his *Total Information Quality Management* (TIQM®)[41] methodology at large telecommunications company in Australia.

Originally published by Larry English as TQdM (total quality data management),[42] TIQM is based on W Edwards Deming's philosophy on quality management, *Total Quality Management (TQM)*, which was adopted widely, especially in manufacturing circles, which is where we first came across TQM. Like TQM, TIQM is a continuous

---

[40] https://tdan.com/interview-with-larry-english/12241.

[41] TIQM is a registered trademark of INFORMATION IMPACT International Inc.

[42] Larry P. English, *Improving Data Warehouse and Business Information Quality, Methods for Reducing Costs and Increasing Profits,* John Wiley and Sons, Inc., 1999.

improvement   approach   to   information   quality
management.[43]

Case study—*TIQM* at a leading telecommunications company

TIQM at a large telecommunications company was responsible for significant improvements to business processes. One example was telephone service fault management. Fixing a reported fault often involved a *truck roll*—sending a technician to the address where the telephone was located. All too often, the technician would arrive to find that no one was home at the address and that the contact telephone number provided was the one with the fault!

Changes were made to the business processes at the call centers, and staff members were educated on the impact of not capturing the correct contact information. Measurement of improvement showed significant reduction in rescheduling truck rolls.

Part of the TIQM approach requires the information quality practitioner to *go to Gemba*—visit the factory floor—to learn and understand the business processes, decision-making, and reasoning behind what data is captured, when, and why.

TIQM is a framework of six continuously cycled processes, labeled P1 through P6. Here's our summary:

---

[43] More information about TIQM at:

http://mitiq.mit.edu/IQIS/Documents/CDOIQS_200977/Papers/01_06_T 2D.pdf.

P1. *Assess Data Definition and Information Architecture Quality*, which is focused on the quality of data models and architectural designs. In manufacturing terms, these are the equivalent of blueprint designs and specifications.

P2. *Assess Information Quality*, which examines how well data aligns against the specifications improved through P1.

P3. *Measure Nonquality [sic] Information Costs*, which evaluates or estimates the cost to the organization due to any particular data quality issue, including lost revenue, direct and indirect costs, potential regulatory risk (fines), and process inefficiencies.

P4. *Reengineer and Cleanse Data*, which employs data quality improvement methods to fix data issues in databases. For example, customer and address matching algorithms to combine duplicate records, and data formatting analysis to identify and rectify incomplete or badly formatted data, such as Social Security Number (SSN) records in the USA or Australian Business Number (ABN) records in Australia.

P5. *Improve Information Process Quality*, in which business processes and reward systems are better aligned to data capture needs. Recall the example in the Case Study—*TIQM* *at* *a* *leading* *telecommunications company.*

P6. *Establish the Information Quality Environment.* Rather than a single process, this is a set of overarching cultural awareness, education, and change management activities that establishes and maintains information-quality principles and way of life for the organization.

For TIQM, or indeed any data quality initiative, to be effective, it must be established holistically, and like any continuous improvement methodology, it requires senior leadership appetite and ongoing investment in resources.

Earlier in this chapter, in the section Business-led information management, *we discussed the return of information management activities to the business community. One option is for the organization to take onboard a business-led information quality methodology such as TIQM.*

We have worked with many clients where we have witnessed data quality initiatives that do not take a holistic approach. Instead, they establish initiatives, and even permanent teams, that focus on cleansing data. We refer to these as cottage industries that continually address the equivalent of the TIQM P4 while the organization ignores the root cause of the problem, which is most often a broken business process. These data cleansing behaviors are systemic of politically motivated organizational cultures, where the cottage industry provides "jobs for life" protection.

"It is difficult to get a man to understand something, when his salary depends upon his not understanding it!"

Upton Sinclair

In the multinational insurance case study presented earlier in this chapter, their focus was on building a technology platform and TIQM P4-type data quality cleansing. The whole project was, in our opinion, based on political agendas rather than prioritized business needs. Also, the focus was on *data* (with our sense of meaning). However, to resolve the commercial team's requirements, *information* was needed from external sources and scanned contracts, and broker agreements would need to be amended.

In summary, the TIQM data quality approach is based on sound principles and starts with clear definition. And to work, it must be implemented holistically.

Software development methodologies

In this section, we look at the different ways our infotech systems are developed and suggest why infotech project failure rates have not improved significantly in decades.

Over the last few decades, we've been actively involved in a range of projects including process control software and system implementations for batch chemical manufacturing, aircraft manufacturing, data warehouse and analytics, dashboard implementations, and web application development. As a result, we have seen two things evolve over time: the software development methodology and, with it, the project life cycle methodology.

But the one thing that we haven't seen change significantly is the number of project failures. So why is that?

Before we answer that question or, at least, give our opinion, we want to reflect on a fundamental reason that has historically caused software project failures. Then we'll explain the characteristics of each of the two main approaches to project life cycle: *waterfall* and *Agile*.

Years ago, a common issue behind project failure, then quoted as being in the region of 40%, was attributed to what is referred to as the *semantic gap*[44]—a breakdown in the

---

[44] We introduced the semantic gap in Chapter 2, *Knowledge*.

process of transferring human knowledge into computer code. In attempts to resolve this issue, many software development methodologies were proposed, such as *Structured analysis and design technique* (SADT), developed in the late 1960s. Other methodologies were developed during the 1970s, such as Ed Yourdon's *Yourdon structured method.* Probably the best-known waterfall method, on which most waterfall methods are based, is *Structured Systems Analysis and Design Method* (SSADM), developed in the 1980s.

Waterfall, as its name suggests, is a one-way flow of processes. The number of stages varies from organization to organization. Still, it generally starts with planning and feasibility, progresses through requirements gathering, and on through the designing, building, testing, and deployment phases. Also known as the System Development Life Cycle (SDLC), it was adopted in the early days of software engineering from the project methodology used in the defense and aerospace industries. However, it has been criticized as inappropriate for software as it does not account for iteration, particularly in the build and test phases, which is not typically needed or desirable in the engineering and construction of physical technology!

Since the mid-1990s, software development methodologies have stressed a more iterative approach. These have been generally referred to since the early 2000s as *Agile*. There have been, and still are, many flavors of Agile frameworks and methodologies, such as Rapid Application

Development, Disciplined Agile Delivery, Scrum, and, most recently, DevOps. The essence, however, of these frameworks is to provide more rapid and incremental delivery and refinement of software. Many organizations have adopted Agile in order to utilize multiple small, cross-functional, dynamic teams.

Despite the move by organizations toward Agile software development, waterfall is still used for larger, more complex system development due to the emphasis on longer analysis and design stages, for example, ERP system configuration and implementation. Waterfall also demands tight controls, both financial and contractual, with funding gates and formal stage sign-offs, which satisfy the needs of high-risk projects.

Waterfall is also used to implement systems that require new infrastructure, such as data and analytics platforms. Once implemented, however, an Agile approach is often applied to the process of delivering new features, fixes, and, in the analytics space, developing tactical business intelligence reports and dashboards, as well as analytical models and insights.

Some organizations implement an incremental development approach that blends waterfall and Agile. This approach uses several small waterfall implementation phases based on a more complete requirements analysis that is performed first. One advantage of this blended approach is that it overcomes the scalability limits of Agile, while satisfying the organization's project funding model having cost-benefits associated with each iteration.

One limitation of Agile has to do with design. Systems that require a focus on data architecture and design often fail under Agile. As mentioned in the *Business Information Models* section, this is because designing a good data model takes time and cannot be decomposed easily. In this situation, the data modeler becomes the bottleneck of the project, and the design work falls into the lap of the software developer, who does not necessarily have the skills of a data modeler. As a result, the software developer creates a physical data model that only suits the immediate needs of the project.

These projects typically involve large data sets and eventually expose the data model's limitations, having evolved over many iterations. The only options left are complex data conversions or code workarounds. These data conversions are often prohibitively expensive, and code workarounds create additional *technical debt* and introduce risk. Building against a compromised design is like building a house of cards.

Ignoring the importance of data modeling and the resulting technical debt is only one reason for eventual project failure. It is simply exacerbating the underlying recurring cause: the semantic gap.

Once again, having a robust set of unambiguous business definitions is a large step in the right direction to reducing the risk of project failure. These definitions can be developed to support Agile software development methods. However, some degree of change is necessary. The definitions must be approved ahead of the sprint that requires them using one of the following approaches:

1. ensure that the definitions are produced during the requirements gathering stage; or
2. utilize a blended software development method to ensure the definitions are produced to support an Agile data modeling process by either:
    a) establishing all the definitions during a first sprint, or
    b) establishing the definitions for a sprint during the previous sprint.

The benefit of the first approach, especially with projects that are developing new infotech, is that known issues relating to the terms being defined will be identified before development begins. The difficulty with the second approach is that it does not sit well with sprint management. (See the case study *Dashboard development without defining terms first* in Chapter 4, *Resources*).

The key take-aways from this section are:

1. one software development method does not fit all;

2. changes are needed to accommodate the development of robust business definitions; and

3. good business definitions should be accessible across projects and reused to reduce the cost associated with not defining, or re-defining, business terms.

Yet organizations will typically favor one method in the same way that they embrace one tool set. Organizations need to choose the appropriate approach to reach the desired outcome.

Case study—Avoiding ineffective infotech investment: tracking adverse events in clinical trials

As organizations grow and look for ways to improve their internal capabilities, they often think the answer is in commercial off-the-shelf (COTS) software packages or outsourced solutions that claim to simplify business processes. These are costly and are not always the right choice. This was the case for one of our clients—a relatively small but growing Australian pharmaceutical research company.

Our client conducted clinical trials in various countries, including Australia, New Zealand, South America, Europe, and the United Kingdom. They were looking to make their product available to the North American market. To market or test a pharmaceutical product in any country, the pharmaceutical company must comply with the local drug regulatory authority, in this case, the FDA (Food and Drug Administration). The FDA has particularly stringent and different requirements for managing what are known as adverse events (AE) and serious adverse events (SAE), particularly under clinical trials.

Our client needed to ensure that any research-related adverse events were reported in accordance with FDA regulations. Non-compliance constitutes a significant risk to the success of a clinical trial and the subsequent registration of the drug for sale in that country. Based on this concern, the staff concluded that the solution was to purchase a fully compliant off-the-shelf adverse event reporting application. The implementation of this new application would also require the migration of their existing adverse event data. Being a small company with few adverse event records, these were managed in a Microsoft Excel workbook.

As a small company, they had limited staff, so we were engaged to manage the project and provide a single point of liaison for the system vendor and our client.

The company used a predominantly paper-based collection method and then entered the information into an Excel workbook for subsequent reporting and tracking purposes. One senior staff member was concerned with the accuracy of the AE data being captured through their current process.

We recommended, as the first step, the evaluation and documentation of the current data capture process, followed by an assessment of the data quality of the AE and SAE data, to ensure a smooth transition to the new system. However, the evaluation of both the business processes and the quality of the captured data uncovered that the business process was the main cause of the data issues.

Although the process was very thorough, it was overly complex. The data quality issues were exacerbated by:

- the inconsistent use of reference data values, such as country codes and SAE classifications, and

- conflicting management accountabilities, such as identifying the responsible party for each step in the process.

We concluded that migrating the existing data and business process to a compliant system would not solve their compliance concerns. Like most transitions to a new system, addressing data quality is not factored into the cost of the data migration—the vendor will usually stipulate that data quality is the client's responsibility. But the client is usually unaware of the data quality issues and their impact to the cost and success of the project. A good vendor will at least recommend a data quality assessment be undertaken to evaluate the cost impact.

After looking at the facts and options, the solution became obvious. The number of serious adverse events over a 3-year period totaled less than 300. The annual subscription cost of the new system was in excess of $140,000 per annum, with a first-year implementation cost of $213,000. That's a 5-year cost of close to a million dollars and a considerable price tag for 100 SAEs/year.

Changes to the business process and modifications to the Excel application were all that was really needed for the company to become compliant. These changes addressed basic information management practices, including security, audit trail, reference data standards, and consistency checking. The process was tightened, the data was repaired, and the new Excel application was implemented.

The Excel application was deemed compliant with the requirements of the FDA and the system originally proposed became unnecessary. Needless to say, the system vendor was not very happy with us! This and subsequent US trials were completed successfully using Excel at a saving in excess of $700,000.

We've seen many organizations jump to expensive technology solutions to address their data issues, often with disastrous results. There are always alternatives, but it is not always obvious what constitutes an appropriate or acceptable alternative.

This pharmaceutical company often refers to us as "our IT guys" and that makes us smile because, as an ex-engineer and ex-accountant, we don't really think of ourselves as IT people; we're business assurance people!

Summary

This chapter provided an overview of data-related topics, including data models, data analytics platform architectures, and data quality. We've also looked at how information management is embedded in IT and why this needs to change for broader information topics. In Chapter 4, *Resources*, we continue with this topic and present an approach that complements IT's data management practices and puts information and knowledge artifact management back in the hands of the business communities.

CHAPTER 4

Resources

This chapter focuses on resources—*information artifacts* that consist of applications that provide visualization of data; policies; data sets in spreadsheets and other file formats; and the written knowledge captured in standard operating procedures and manuals. We need to manage and govern these information artifacts differently from data.

Rather than starting this chapter with a simple quote, we want to share an excerpt from an interview we conducted with the chief financial officer of a large university. This is typical of the point of view that we hear from finance and risk management department leaders.

Interview between a university CFO, Mark Atkins, and Terry Smith—20 July 2019.

Question: *Who do you believe is responsible for the quality of information at the university? If everyone, do you think it needs to be coordinated?*

CFO: *Finance (CFO) via [the Chief Data and Analytics Officer] is responsible. Everybody plays a part, but we need a process for assuring, coordination, and stewardship—[there are] different accountabilities for different data sets.*

Question: *Do you think you can have great quality data and still have poor information quality?*

CFO: *No not necessarily… better data leads to better information; with good data you're more likely to have good information.*

Question: *Do you think business language affects information quality?*

CFO: *Yes.*

Question: *How much effort does your team put into month-end reporting (data processing)? Has it ever been measured?*

CFO: *Loads… lot of time. We have 260 business analysts in this organization… 80% are wrangling data and not analyzing. [And that's just the] tip of the iceberg.*

Question: *What keeps you awake at night? What are your major pain points?*

CFO: *There are data sets out there that we don't know about. Knowing we are 100% fulfilling regulatory* *obligations in such a large organization with a complex, changing landscape, [I question] will changes endure? … With people leaving, is it embedded in BAU [business-as-usual]?*

Question: *Finally, what do you think the biggest opportunity is?*

CFO: *Also that we have data sets out there we don't know about. They could be really valuable.*

In light of the many data breaches being reported around the world, the most notable in Australia at the time of writing in 2022 being Optus (a telecommunications company), the last two answers sum up for us the fact that data stored outside of databases as information can be a liability for an organization, rather than an asset as preached by infotech vendors, unless appropriately curated and governed. Unfortunately, that's not often the case.

Therefore, this chapter will provide guidance for the effective business management and governance of information artifacts, creating a business-as-usual (BAU) discipline that shifts the focus away from, but is complementary to, the processes of utilizing data.

Our objective is to show you how to measure the cost and value of your organizational resources and apply the KSIR principles to both the maintenance of existing artifacts and the specification and development of new artifacts.

At the end of the chapter, armed with the knowledge gleaned from the previous chapters, you should have a framework on which to capture and build organizational capability that will enable you to operate effectively and to make informed investment in infotech.

The cost of poor information resource management

Are you aware of how much your organization spends on stale or copied data and information? Not just in the hardware, which is, of course, getting cheaper each year, but also in the time and effort taken by the hunter-gatherers who compile reports and perform month-end processing, or staff who just have difficulty finding that document or spreadsheet they need.

A study by International Data Corporation (IDC) in 2018 found that data professionals are losing 50% of their time every week—30% searching for and preparing data, plus 20% duplicating work.[45]

---

[45] *The State of Data Discovery and Cataloging,* An IDC Infobrief, 2018 www.forbes.com/sites/forbestechcouncil/2019/12/17/reality-check-still-spending-more-time-gathering-instead-of-analyzing/?sh=352ccca28ffa.

Of course, there is also the problem of maintaining records of certain information, such as email conversations, for statutory periods, especially in government organizations. But the real headache here is knowing what must be kept or archived and what can be destroyed.

One of the mistakes organizations make is trying to handle the masses of information artifacts through complex search systems. However, these technical approaches do not address the root cause, so they should not be considered the solution to the problem. The KSIR strategy is a viable alternative for addressing the root cause of artifact mismanagement. It enables the process of exposing valuable information artifacts while identifying the worthless or undependable—sorting the wheat from the chaff.

Artifact management and the business encyclopedia

Resources are the final stage of the KSIR strategy to managing risk. In Chapter 1, *Knowledge*, we looked at the importance of clear definition of the business concepts that we use in our everyday communication. This is part of the *know what*. We need to expand the management of the *know what* to include other important explicit knowledge that is captured in artifacts.

But knowing *what* is just the beginning. We also need to know *who, when, where, and why,* before we can improve and maintain tacit knowledge—*know how.*

Our company is driven by the core principle that everyone should have access to what they need to succeed. For us, this means that everyone has access to the organizational community support, which we covered in Chapter 2, *Sociality,* and also easy access to reliable *information and knowledge artifacts,* such as dashboards, reports, data sets, standard operating procedures, policies, strategic initiative statements, web pages (both internal and external), etc. In other words, access to anything that helps support our sense of purpose and position within the team and the activities we must perform.

A common complaint we hear from our clients is that their document management (also called knowledge management) systems are difficult to use; that finding an artifact is like a treasure hunt. We will examine the reasons why this might be later in the chapter.

It is impossible to put a cost on the time employees spend hunting and gathering. If you look at your own experience and ask your staff for their estimate, the time will likely be a significant number of hours per week. Of course, one would hope that the front-line operations staff have easy access to very clear operating procedures. But are their performance metrics conducive to capturing the quality of information that you and others need to succeed? (See *Data and Information Quality* under Chapter 3, *Infotech*.)

We recommend that you utilize the knowledge gleaned from this and the previous chapters to create your organization's *business encyclopedia*. This is a central register that is accessible by everyone, easy to use, and provides details about important information artifacts (details that IT would call *business metadata*):

- what the artifact contains (synopsis),
- what kind of artifact it is,
- where it is located,
- who created it,
- when it was created,
- why it was created (the project reference),
- who the curator is,
- what issues exist that may affect its useability,
- when it was last reviewed,
- what business terms are referenced,
- what other artifacts are referenced by it,
- who uses it on a regular basis,
- how often it is used,
- how sensitive it is, and
- what stage of its life cycle it is in—approved for use, in review, suggested, etc.

We won't be discussing aspects of access, such as sensitivity and security, as we expect access to be managed by whatever repository stores the artifact. However, we will discuss the current drivers for documenting *critical data elements* and an approach that utilizes the KSIR strategy.

The business encyclopedia is a register of all important resources: people, artifacts, issues, business term definitions, and related projects. But it is also a means to establish and measure the governance of those resources. However, before we talk about resource governance, we must decide what to govern.

What to govern—data and information artifacts

Before discussing governance over data or information, we need to revisit one of the general principles introduced in Chapter 3, *Infotech*, section *Data and Information Quality*.

Our personal preference is to use the term "data" when referring to structured, machine-readable forms, and the term "information" as a broader term that extends into the world of what is called unstructured data or semi-structured data by the information technologists, such as documents and reports, etc. *We* refer to these as information artifacts.

Research done at Monash University in Melbourne, Australia on information governance (their terminology) showed the question over "what to govern" to be one of the biggest factors of failed governance strategies.[46] Incidentally, at the time of writing, we believe this research to be the only academic research into information governance! The results of that research suggest three angles from which to view information and apply governance. [47] One angle offered is format-based— governing structured data or higher-level information (unstructured data). Another angle presented is content-based—classifying data by business concepts. These two angles align well with our experience, using business concepts and managing data and information separately. (The third, taxonomy-based angle, offers four ways of viewing types of data.)

The governance of information artifacts is something that we've rarely seen done successfully. Certain industry verticals are quite good at it, like those in the legal, finance, and medical professions. Others are not. As data governance has been a trend for many years now, especially in response to new regulatory demands, why do

---

[46] Sindy Madrid-Torus, *The conceptualisation and implementation of information governance: A design-science approach*, Monash University, 2014.

[47] Practice Guide – Information Governance: What is it? How to implement it? (Part of the doctoral research by Sindy Madrid-Torus, The conceptualisation and implementation of information governance: A design-science approach, Monash University, 2014).

organizations struggle with this? One reason is that organizations cannot decide what to govern and become overwhelmed in trying to establish complex overarching frameworks—again, influenced by vendor-told best practice!

We recommend using your business glossary of business terms to capture the assignment of accountability and responsibility for the terms and their definitions. This assignment can then cascade to any data closely related to that business term. Also, information artifacts require their own governance structure, for which we recommend a hierarchy of curated sections within libraries that are aligned to the major business functions (usually between 12 and 20) and assigning accountability and responsibility to these.

While many IT professionals have tried to align ownership or stewardship by data subject areas (*domains*), such as customer and product, the truth is that data associated with these subjects is too broadly used across the organization. However, if you get down to specific customer and product attributes, the ownership decision becomes clearer, and can be applied to a functional area. For example, an organization may have retail and corporate customers, each managed by different functional areas. Trying to apply accountability for both under a *customer domain* will obviously not be successful.

A huge benefit of applying ownership at the business functional area is that business functions are stable while organizational structures are continually changing. And when you get down to the nitty-gritty of who *owns* specific data and information, by establishing ownership of the actual business term, its definition, and its valid values, you will find that responsibility of the associated data and information will fall in the laps of those same stakeholders.

As an example, we conducted some workshops with an Australian telecommunications company that was establishing a single billing platform to be shared with its overseas parent company. Once we got to the specifics of the definition for "retail customer account," the legal implications that were revealed through the rules embedded in the definition caught the attention of the legal representative in the workshop, who insisted that they own the definition and should "own" (have final say over) the use of retail customer account data.

In summary, we believe that successful ownership and governance requires a business functional division and a careful definition of the governance terms, such as "owner," "steward," "curator," etc. It also follows that, if you can get ownership of the term and its definition, the ownership of the associated information and data will follow more naturally.

Be aware that sometimes the ownership of data is at the individual value level. An example is the case study that we presented in Chapter 1, *Knowledge, Make the intangible tangible: measure project time spent on definitions*, where we found that the individual brand managers each had ownership (decision rights) over subsets of the brand values, although their superior had final say over the definition of "brand" for that company.

Critical data elements and data catalogs

Many regulatory bodies now require organizations to identify their *critical data elements* (CDEs). The intent is to provide an organization with a *focused* risk management approach to governing its data. After all, how can an organization make good business decisions based on questionable data? And how can regulatory bodies believe that the organization's regulatory submissions are trustworthy?

Both regulations and the "data-driven" mantra have driven organizations to invest a great deal of time and energy trying to identify critical data elements, not only to be compliant, but also to prioritize their data management efforts and better utilize their limited resources. Some organizations consider this CDE requirement a starting point for data governance.

There is a very large number of data elements in numerous data repositories that exist in organizations, and the volume grows daily. Therefore, identifying critical data elements is an enormous task to undertake, especially if the approach is to evaluate each data element against some set of criteria to determine which of them are critical.

> *We should ask ourselves, "Is this the best way to focus our data risk management efforts? Does all this effort bring value to the organization, or is it a tick in the box?"*

How does one identify a critical data element? Let's start with a definition. Many can be found on the internet, but all are variations of:

> *"Data that is vital to the successful operation of the organization."*
> **David Loshin, 2009**

As you can see from the date it was written, this concept is not new. How do the regulatory bodies define what a critical data element is? Well, as usual, they're a bit vague. They don't actually define what one is, just that they are at the core of data risk management and should be determined by the requirements of the business. It is left to the individual organization to define what a critical data element is. Once again, the infotech vendors are vying to sell their data catalogs as a means to label CDEs.

APRA, the Australian Prudential Regulatory Authority, is the statutory authority that regulates the Australian financial services industry. They recommend that organizations should consider two things when identifying critical data elements: 1) their usage, and 2) their impact on the business, from aspects such as legal, financial, and regulatory.

From the following case study, you will see that defining your key business terms is a more effective top-down approach to begin identifying CDEs.

Case study—Identifying CDEs for a multinational insurance company

We were engaged by a multinational insurance company to define key business terms and create the core of an enterprise logical data model, which was reviewed against an insurance industry model from the Association for Cooperative Operations Research and Development (ACORD). The head of data strategy and governance championed the objective. Having successfully completed the objective, her team then populated the definitions and the data model into their data governance tool (IBM Infosphere), and they planned to begin mapping these business terms, entities, and attributes, to the data elements in their systems. They then requested that we perform a second round of workshops with the same business stakeholders to identify CDEs and classify them according to a number of criteria:

1. Is it personal identity information (PII)?
2. Is it required for regulatory compliance?
3. Is it used for external reporting?

4. Is it used for internal reporting (financial, operational, management)?
5. Is it used to calculate key performance indicators?
6. Is it used for operational processing?
7. Is it used for analysis or decision-making?
8. Is it key master data (customer, product, supplier)?

The key questions asked to identify an attribute or term as critical were:

1. Will the loss of the data cause business disruption?
2. Will the loss or disclosure of the data cause reputational harm?
3. Will the loss or poor quality of the data cause loss of revenue?
4. Will the loss or poor quality of the data cause bad customer experience?

It is important to remember that what is critical to one person, team, department, or division, may not be important to another.

Results: Of the core data model's 266 attributes that were analyzed against the CDE criteria, all but 32 ticked the box for at least one criterion. Of those 32, most were internal department codes or status codes, none of which had been defined as key business terms.

We've been asked to identify CDEs for other organizations with the same result. Also note that, when looking at data elements rather than business concepts, identifying a single data element as critical is a flawed approach. Take birthdate, for example. Birthdate alone can be seen as not critical, but in connection with the person to which it belongs, it becomes critical personal identity information (PII). The set of data together provides the context and creates the risk to the organization (and possibly the individual).

As a final consideration, should an organization collect and store information if it is not critical to their organization?

Business-driven, not data-driven

As well as deciding what information resources to govern, and where to expend effort, it's important to consider how to implement information management as a business function and what aspects of this need governance.

In Chapter 2, *Sociality*, we discussed the importance of having *visibility* of business issues and concerns, and an organizational culture that rewards, or at least does not marginalize, those who raise their issues and concerns. Your business encyclopedia must include a register for issues and a registration process that is accessible to all.

One of the key difficulties we encountered in establishing TIQM at a large telecommunications company was the overwhelming number of issues that started landing in the information quality email account's inbox. We had to establish some form of gating process. We recommend that any issue, if sufficiently considered, can be categorized by a single business term. If that term has not been defined, then it must first be suggested for inclusion in the encyclopedia. Once suggested, the governance community can prioritize the terms in line with the severity of the issue and begin the definition and issue resolution process.

Don't be tempted to use your IT case management system as an information issue register because the staff behind that process will likely be incentivized to close tickets within a short period, probably driven by some service-level agreement. Information issues will take much longer to solve and must be prioritized by the governance team.

By prioritizing business issues, which may include concerns over available information, errors in information artifacts, and broken or inefficient business processes, the governance team can establish a taskforce. A taskforce is one of the communities of practice that we introduced in Chapter 2, *Sociality*, that resolve the most important issues. Informed decisions can be made from the results of each step of the process:

1. Identify and define the stakeholders affected by the issue.

2. Understand the cost implications.

3. Identify the terminology at the heart of the issue and establish who will be accountable (the *business owner*).

4. Establish the business glossary community of practice (or working group) for the related terms to include the stakeholders and the specialist analysts, such as definition authors, facilitators, and curators.

5. Define the terminology at the heart of the issue.

6. Establish the measures for success.

7. Provide clear requirements for the resolution of the issue.

8. Track and report progress.

9. Maintain all associated entries in the business encyclopedia (the issue should already be registered):

    a. the resolution's project information,
    b. business term definition life cycle stage,
    c. stakeholder map,
    d. associated artifacts, and
    e. the relationships between the above.

10. Record the estimated year-on-year savings—use this information to showcase the benefits.

11. Reward the team and those who raise issues.

The governance team should establish a reward system and they should be empowered and funded appropriately. The reward process should form part of their *terms of reference*.

Resource accountability and responsibility

Establishing a suitable structure for organizing your business encyclopedia is key to enabling the business community and governance management. It has to support their needs, not the needs of the data management group, who are primarily concerned with data catalogs that document data elements and *lineage*. (Lineage is how data moves through the organization's systems.) These data catalogs might look appropriate for use as an encyclopedia, but they usually require a deep understanding of the terminology used in the systems that they are cataloging. *Figure 5* shows how we structure our encyclopedia. It also shows how we apply accountability and responsibility to the encyclopedia's content.

Since the names used for information and data governance vary between organizations, you must adopt names that are not confusing. We've seen the names *owner, custodian, steward, business steward, data steward*, etc., adopted from various *data* governance practitioners and infotech vendors.

The names *we* use for our encyclopedia roles are:

- *Head Librarian* — a person who is accountable for the registration of content within their *Library*. There can only be one Head Librarian for a Library. They have approval rights over content, including definitions.

- *Librarian*—a person who is responsible for managing the content of a Library. There can be more than one Librarian assigned to a Library and a person may be a Librarian for more than one Library. They have review rights over content.

- *Curator*—a person responsible for managing *Sections* of *Artifacts* within a Library and verifying conformity of the registered artifacts.

- *Author*— a person who is specialized in writing definitions to your adopted standard.

- *Stakeholder*—a person who has consultation rights over content quality.

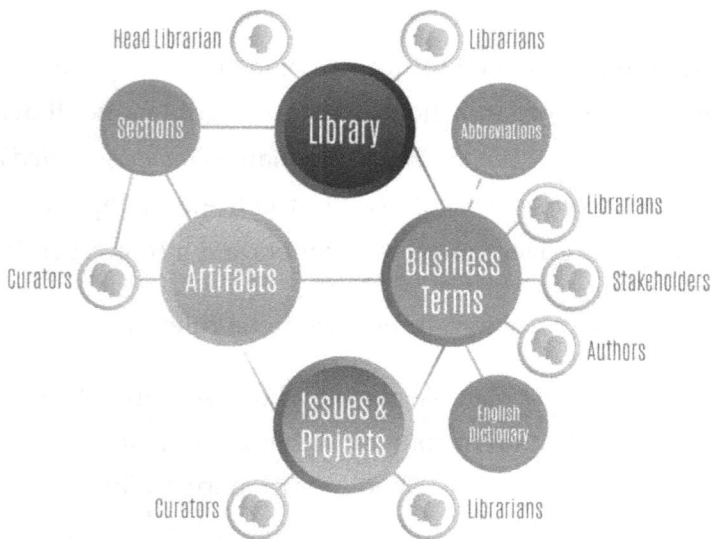

Figure 5—Example Encyclopedia Structure

Another important point about accountability is ensuring it extends into infotech project teams. This is ideally done by communicating the existence of your business terms and artifact register (business encyclopedia) to the business analysts and project managers, especially those engaged via vendors. In the case of vendors, their payment criteria should include registration of project documentation (artifacts) to the satisfaction of the assigned curator. This will also ensure alignment with the definitions in the glossary component of the encyclopedia.

Some organizations, particularly in the government sector, do not like to use the term "owner" because they believe that the true owner is the external citizen that provided the data. It's important to establish which of the people within your organization will be held accountable for their sets of artifacts and term definitions.

The following case study is an example of the situation caused by not defining dashboard terminology.

Case study—Dashboard development without defining terms first

The data and analytics department of an Australian university launched a number of concurrent projects to build dashboards for various areas across the university. This was a considerable undertaking to be completed in a very limited time, thus requiring multiple teams to work concurrently.

These dashboards would provide insights into various areas across the university. They would enable the analysis of: courses, student recruitment and admissions, student demographics and engagement, and student success. They would also provide metrics on staff movements, attrition, and leave.

The multiple business intelligence (BI) development teams worked in isolation, each deciding the name displayed for a given metric or dimension on their dashboard; the name sometimes being based on the data engineer's interpretation of the data they found in the source. Many of the dashboard terms and metrics were not defined. What happens when terms and metrics are not defined?

When the dashboards were presented to the stakeholders, many inconsistencies were identified, for example, some of the same key terms were labeled differently in each dashboard and had different displayed values. Subsequently, workshops had to be conducted with the stakeholders, leading to rework that could have been avoided. For example, one dashboard provided incorrect metrics based on an assumption of the meaning of the source data. The business stakeholders recognized this immediately and requested the metrics to be taken out of the dashboard, a clear case of wasted development effort—scrap and rework!

The university had (and still has) a well-established glossary of business terms and definitions that are managed by a governance community. Their business glossary has the capability of providing definitions via application programming interfaces (APIs) to their dashboards. The available terms and definitions are even published dynamically to the university's policy website, a key resource for students and staff alike. But, as the project did not define the terms and did not follow the glossary governance process, definitions were not available from the glossary for the users of the dashboards.

The university has since implemented dashboard quality measures in their project delivery process.

> **Define your business terms first before the development of dashboards begins.**

Information governance function—CFO, CRO, COO, or PMO

You should be convinced by now that the information governance structure we are recommending does not sit well under your IT department. We have seen many failed information governance initiatives and one thing they all have in common is that they were initiated by, or were usurped by, IT. Certainly, many elements of data management belong under the direction of the CIO, but the broader information management and information governance must include broader organizational buy-in.

So, from where should information governance be championed? In Chapter 3, *Infotech*, we suggested that information governance would sit well under the CFO, CRO, or COO. We have seen successful information governance groups that have been positioned under the CFO, particularly when the CFO includes a department that provides an operational reporting function. We also believe that the operations group is a good spot to drive information governance, because they are closest to the operational headaches and are, therefore, better equipped to call priorities and find funding. But assuming that the

CIO sits under the COO, why does information governance not sit well under the CIO?

The answer may be to do with the fact that IT operates as a service organization and relies heavily on the ability to charge back or capitalize their funding. This comes down to the organization's funding model and accounting principles. They are also typically divided into an enterprise architecture (EA) area and separately managed development and operational support areas. The EA area is overly driven by opinion and is a cost organization, while the development area relies on project funding.

All the operational system implementation projects we've seen requiring data migration ended up vastly over budget and time. This is because the vendor always makes the client contractually responsible for data quality. The data quality remediation is never sufficiently covered by the budget because the client doesn't have the capability. So, data quality gets pushed into the "we'll do it later" phase that usually never occurs. So once again, your staff will have to deal with the problems, requiring costly workarounds and reducing job satisfaction. This often leads to the creation or expansion of that data quality cottage industry we introduced in Chapter 3, Infotech, under Data and Information Quality!

With the latest trend of organizational transformation being driven by the disruptive threats which we briefly mentioned in the introduction to Chapter 3, *Infotech*, we suggest that the project management office (PMO) is a good place to consider establishing a head of information governance. Although information governance and project governance are not the same; they should work hand in hand. For example, any project that includes data or information should have data quality measures attached to their success criteria.

Most project documentation includes valuable artifacts and definitions that never see the light of day after the project is finished. For all those definitions that business analysts write, we suspect that few are reused on other projects implementing the same concepts, even if you have a central glossary. Repeated effort expended on defining the same terms will continue to happen until definition reuse is measured and the use of a central business glossary is mandated. Also, each project must have sufficient funding to define any new terms to an appropriate quality standard.

So, in summary, consider establishing your information governance with the CFO, as part of the PMO or transformation office, or better yet, under the Chief Risk Officer (CRO), where it can be aligned with *business governance*—but never as part of an IT group.

Beyond artifact management—content reuse

Assuming you have begun to implement artifact management within your area of the organization, or across the whole organization, your community of practice should be finding and registering artifacts that they deem important for the effective running of the organization. Expanding upon the artifact types we mentioned before, the list includes:

- *Documents*—specifications, policies, procedures, certificates, white papers, training manuals, confluent pages or spaces, intranet pages, presentations, etc.—anything that can instruct a team member in the operation of a business process or provide information on business activities. An example might be a staff onboarding procedure on your Culture and People department's intranet site, or your trademark certificates.

- *Data sets*—spreadsheets, department databases, SharePoint lists, etc.—anything that provides information that supports or reports on a business process. An example might be a supplier list, an in-flight project list in the finance department's network file storage, or a quarterly sales report.

- *Dashboards*—any reporting application viewed through a visualization tool, such as Tableaux,

Power BI, Qlik, Zoho, Domo, etc., that provides historical analysis, trending, and forecasting of operational data.

- *Multimedia*—videos, audio clips, photographs, interactive learning modules, etc.

Regardless of where the artifact is stored, there should be a central register as part of your business encyclopedia. This should be accessible to anyone and be easily found. Remember that the access and security controls are managed by the owners of the storage platform, not in the register. The main objectives are eliminating duplicates, promoting reuse, efficient search across storage platforms, and capturing and uplifting functional knowledge.

Many organizations do not have fully documented procedures, even for some of their most basic processes. Part of building your curators' capability includes capturing and verifying standard operating procedures. This may sound like a daunting and time-consuming activity, but there's a simple method that we use called SYSTEMology[48] that makes the task quick and effective.

Your artifact storage platform will likely not be a single technology. Most organizations we've worked with have at

---

[48] David Jenyns, *SYSTEMology: Create Time, Reduce Errors and Scale Your Profits with Proven Business Systems*, SYSTEMology, 2020.

least four, such as Microsoft SharePoint (including Teams), Atlassian Confluence, an intranet, and a storage area network (SAN). And you'll also likely have printed storage in file cabinets. All of these will have some form of location, either a uniform resource locator (URL) or a physical cabinet reference, which will be the unique identifier for the artifact's location.

Once you've established who in your department will be responsible for the curation of the artifacts, you should be able to measure their performance in this role. For example, you might measure in a reporting period:

- artifacts registered,
- artifacts due for review and reviewed on time,
- issues raised against their artifacts, and
- comments or likes from the community against their artifacts.

The curation process should also be recording:

- business terms referenced by the artifact and level of compliance to the definitions of those business terms (linking the artifact register to the glossary components of your business encyclopedia);
- artifact dependencies, for example policy documents usually reference other policies, which provide a means of identifying the impact of any changes to cross-referenced artifacts; and
- the project or activity that created the artifact.

Linking business terms to artifacts provides scope and clarity of the artifact content. It also improves search ability for your artifact repositories. Another valuable feature is the dynamic reuse of business glossary content.

For example, linking the set of business terms to a dashboard artifact will, via an application programming interface (API), allow the dashboard user to dynamically retrieve the appropriate list of terms and definitions from the glossary. Therefore, the dashboard's definitions are always up to date. In the same way, when creating Microsoft Word documents that require a glossary as part of the content, the definitions can be embedded as a link to the API, just like linking a video.

The following case study is a great example of how establishing a community of practice, as a business function with a common language, enabled a Fortune 500 telecommunication company, operating in the Asia Pacific region, to create and manage an infotech resource that was crucial to regulatory reporting—one that their Information Technology Services (ITS) department had continually failed to deliver. This led to the company achieving increased confidence in business decision-making, reducing regulatory risk, and finding and eliminating unseen revenue leakage.

Case study—Seven different numbers for one metric

It all started with the Chief Financial Officer (CFO) who was frustrated because he was getting seven conflicting numbers for a key reporting metric. This metric, a count of "basic telephone services," is reported to the government in compliance with the universal service obligation. It's also used to apportion power consumption costs, calculate associated greenhouse gas emissions, and for operational reporting of revenue and churn.

Every reporting period involved a huge number of people and a considerable effort in cross-checking the numbers as well as trying to understand why those numbers conflicted with each other.

The ITS area had already executed several projects over several years, at significant cost (millions of dollars), in attempts to fix the problem, but with no success. These projects focused on building reporting processes that would bring together data from the many systems needed to perform the complex processes of ordering, activating, and billing telephone services. In other words, the ITS solutions focused on automating the reporting process without understanding the data or being knowledgeable about the associated business processes.

Enter the Chief Data Officer (CDO), a new role that was implemented as part of a program for cultural change, with a focus on information quality. After much research, the CDO chose the Total Information Quality Management (TIQM) methodology developed by Larry English. (See Chapter 3, *Infotech, Data and Information Quality*.) We were brought in to help solve the CFO's basic telephone service headache. Using a combination of the TIQM methodology and our methodology, we thoroughly analyzed the reporting environment.

We found a staggeringly complex interaction of people processes, operational systems, and data. In fact, there were 17 different people-based processes and 12 different systems, each of which introduced its own set of problems. This meant that the final combined figures had deeply compounded problems. This was why it took an alarmingly heavy use of resources to try and track the cause of discrepancies and perform the necessary estimations and adjustments.

Once we had figured out how and, just as importantly, when the raw data was being moved around and processed, it was a relatively easy job to intercept the necessary data sets. We then established an analytics environment ("the sandpit") in which we could begin our investigation and understand the nuances of the data. Now it was time to establish a community of practice by bringing key people together. The people involved in managing, provisioning, activating, billing, and reporting the basic telephone service product were spread across many departments and regions. However, with the mandate from the CFO and CDO, we were able to identify key stakeholders and subject matter experts in order to establish a governance working group to oversee their specific business information needs and issues. Through a number of regional meetings and workshops, using video conferencing where face-to-face workshops were not possible, we began to educate the community in basic information quality principles, lead them to appreciate and resolve the underlying language problems, and facilitate the exchange of knowledge around the problem area.

This is what we discovered. A basic telephone service could be provided in a number of guises, depending on the combination of facilities the service was configured to provide. The configuration was stored as values in eight different data fields, with groups of permutations constituting a "product." Products included: active lines that only allowed emergency calls, private lines, public telephones, shared lines, groups of lines for small businesses, pricing options, voicemail, etc. And there were differing opinions as to which products were considered basic telephone services. This last point was the main reason why different numbers were being reported, compounded by the difficulty in identifying the product configurations within and across the systems.

Through the workshops, we defined and agreed what a basic telephone service was for reporting purposes. We agreed on the term name, "basic telephone service - service in operation" (BTS-SIO), to differentiate the installed services term from those services being billed as a basic telephone service. Next came the job of defining how to translate the eight field value combinations to identify the right combinations. This was not a simple task. One of the fields was supposed to be the main product identifier, but it had been used randomly to carry unrelated encoded information, such as "customer has a dog that bites" and "customer only speaks Portuguese." These other codes were probably important for the customer support or field technicians but created a significant hurdle when trying to identify the basic telephone services. And there were over 10,000 values in the list, a number that was ever growing!

We established a process for tracking the addition of new values and established governance roles within the community to be responsible for managing these values. Working closely with the governance community, we were able to classify all 10,000 and establish the rules for identifying a basic telephone service. With a single agreed definition for a basic telephone service and the rules to translate the data into information, we were then able to identify $1.5M annual revenue leakage. For example, where a telephone service was provisioned but wasn't being billed. We were also able to identify and rectify other quality problems, such as resolving situations where services were being incorrectly billed and the customer's bill was in dispute. So, how long did this take and how much did it cost? About three months and a few hundred thousand dollars of additional resource costs. The costs included new data feeds and one full-time resource to coordinate the ongoing reporting and quality activities. As for the other resources, it was just a matter of realigning the duties of the product managers and subject matter experts involved in the ongoing governance processes for basic telephone service. In essence, the company now had a community of practice capable of performing effective information management outside of the IT department.

As an epilogue, the Enterprise Architecture department insisted that the basic telephone service reports (from the sandpit) needed to be implemented under their reporting platform architecture in order to become a production system maintained by ITS. So, reluctantly, a project was formed at a cost to the business of more than two million dollars and, as we learned several years later, it did not deliver, was over budget, and our "sandpit" continued to produce the reporting for the CFO for several years. (We explored one of the underlying reasons in Chapter 3, *Infotech*, *Industry Data Models*.)

We think there's a lesson here in challenging the CIO about who is better able to perform information management, and the real cost of their complex IT systems and ineffective vendor management model, all of which were revealed as contributing factors in a BTS-SIO project risk evaluation.

Summary

This chapter has expanded on information management as a business function. With a focus on managing artifacts, we discussed artifact curation and governance, and a method of structuring the roles and responsibilities using a library model. Combining artifact registration with the knowledge captured through definition workshops (Chapter 2, *Sociality*), we presented the concept of an business encyclopedia as a means of capturing and sharing knowledge, prioritizing and solving business issues that are aligned with business strategy, and measuring the effectiveness of the governance management.

Summary

"Insanity is repeating the same mistakes and expecting different results."

Narcotics Anonymous, 1981[49]

We hope by now you are at least questioning whether your organization's investment in data and analytics is appropriately informed and achieving the promised objectives. Perhaps you're already asking those difficult questions, or perhaps you're not convinced that the vendors' "data-driven" mantra is misleading your infotech staff?

Whatever you believe, new or unchanged, we thank you for reading this far and hope you have gained benefit from doing so.

Here's a quick recap of the four-point KSIR strategy—Knowledge, Sociality, Infotech, and Resources—that must

---

[49] A similar quote, "the definition of insanity is doing the same thing over and over and expecting different results," as used in Chapter 4, is often attributed to Albert Einstein, although there's no evidence he ever said that.

be supported by four *abilities*—Visibility; Capability; Accountability; and Measurability.

Chapter 1, *Knowledge*—dealt with finding those knowledgeable in the organization, capturing and sharing their knowledge through a process of workshops, and using structured definitions to provide clarity. Of the four abilities, the key here is *capability*.

Chapter 2, *Sociality*—dealt with building organization sociality through principles, contracts, and processes that are simple and easy to follow, provide a sense of purpose and fulfillment, and lead to work-life improvements. Of the four abilities, the key points here are *visibility* and *accountability*.

Chapter 3, *Infotech*—examined aspects of data-related information technology and methods for communicating effectively about infotech needs, so that they can be cost-effectively fulfilled and strategically aligned. Of the four abilities, the key points here are *measurability* and *accountability*.

Chapter 4, *Resources*—presented the final point with the ongoing collation, curation, and publication of information resources (artifacts), so everyone can access what they need to succeed. All four abilities, *capability*, *visibility*, *measurability*, and *accountability*, are key points here.

In the final chapter, we also introduced the concept of an *business encyclopedia* that facilitates the KSIR strategy and the performance measures of your organization's information management ecosystem. We provided recommendations on information governance structures that support and reward your communities of practice. We also recommended that an information and knowledge governance initiative should not be managed under IT's data governance umbrella.

Being *data-driven* is not a sustainable approach to improving business. Instead, capturing and nurturing the knowledge of the organization creates a *business-driven* approach that is a good risk mitigation strategy for:

- ensuring regulatory compliance,
- making informed infotech investment,
- preventing loss of organizational knowledge due to staff attrition, and
- delivering reliable information.

As a final note, this approach should never be considered a *project*. It is a business-as-usual set of processes that must be adopted, funded, and committed to by the senior leadership team.

Figure 6 provides a high-level overview of the four-point KSIR strategy.

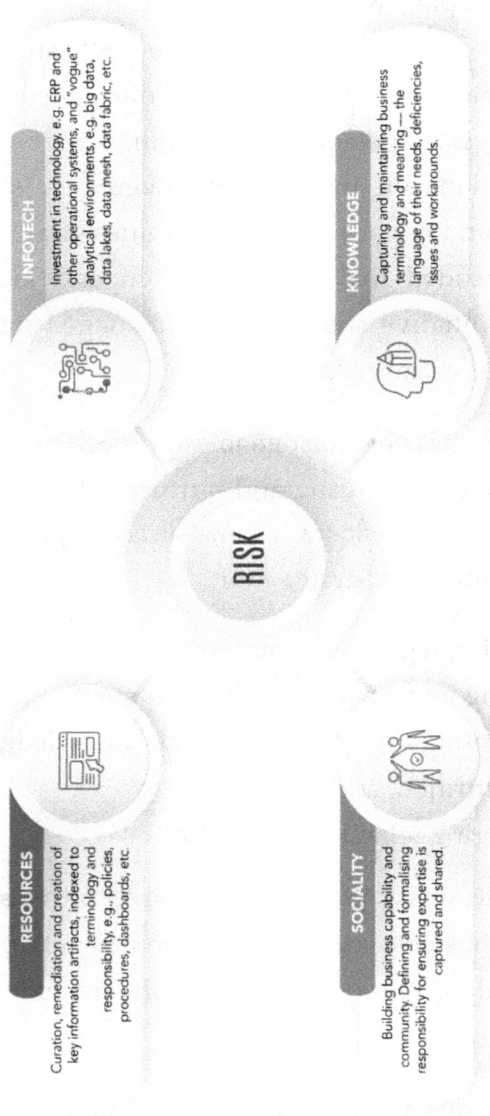

Figure 6—the four points of the KSIR strategy for mitigating risk.

INFOTECH

Investment in technology, e.g. ERP and other operational systems, and "vogue" analytical enviornments, e.g. big data, data lakes, data mesh, data fabric, etc.

KNOWLEDGE

Capturing and maintaining business terminology and meaning — the language of their needs, deficiencies, issues and workarounds.

RISK

RESOURCES

Curation, remediation and creation of key information artifacts, indexed to terminology and responsibility, e.g., policies, procedures, dashboards, etc.

SOCIALITY

Building business capability and community. Defining and formalising responsibility for ensuring expertise is captured and shared.

Further Reading

Chapter 1:

My Grammar and I (or Should That Be 'Me'?), Caroline Taggart and J. A. Wines, Michael O'Mara Books Limited, 2020

Chapter 2:

Tribes, We Need You to Lead Us, Seth Godin, Piatkus (UK) / Portfolio (USA), 2008.

Chapter 3:

Does IT Matter?, Nicholas G. Carr, Harvard Business School Publishing Corporation, 2004.

Improving Data Warehouse and Business Information Quality, Larry P. English, John Wiley & Sons, Inc., 1999.

Chapter 4:

SYSTEMology: Create Time, Reduce Errors and Scale Your Profits with Proven Business Systems, David Jenyns, SYSTEMology, 2020.

Index

www.ingramcontent.com/pod-product-compliance
Lightning Source LLC
Chambersburg PA
CBHW071607210326
41597CB00019B/3441